How To Get A Man Without Getting Played

29 Dating Secrets to Catch Mr. Right, Set Your Standards, and Eliminate Time Wasters

D0034010

By Bruce Bryans

Legal Disclaimer

Although the author and publisher have made every effort to ensure that the information in this book was correct at press time, the author and publisher do not assume and hereby disclaim any liability to any party for any loss, damage, or disruption caused by errors or omissions, whether such errors or omissions result from negligence, accident, or any other cause. This publication is solely for personal growth and is sold with the understanding that neither the author nor the publisher is engaged in presenting professional advice. Nor is anything in this book intended to be a diagnosis, prescription, recommendation, or cure for any specific kind of psychological, sexual, or medical problem.

ISBN-13: 978-1545582909

ISBN-10: 1545582904

My Free Gift to You

As a way of saying "thanks" for your purchase, I'm offering a free 10-lesson email course (and other assorted goodies) that are exclusive to my book readers. Each lesson reveals some of my best-kept dating secrets for cultivating **long-term attraction** with high-quality men.

You can access it at:

http://www.brucebryans.com/ecourse/

In this free course, you will not only learn the most high-value dating behaviors that make men burn with desire and desperate to commit to a woman, but you'll also learn how to confidently interact with men so that you can get the guy you want, keep him interested, and quickly weed out time-wasters, players, and men who'll never commit.

Again, you can access it at:

http://www.brucebryans.com/ecourse/

Table of Contents

Introduction *1*

Chapter One: How to Date a Man to Get His Love and Respect..*9*

Chapter Two: Power Dating Strategies for finding Mr. Right *37*

Chapter Three: The Beliefs and Standards of High-Value Women *67*

Chapter Four: How to Capture His Heart and Bring Out His Best *91*

Final Thoughts...*111*

"If men knew what women really thought regarding love and sex, they would be twice as bold in their pursuit. If women knew what men really thought regarding love and sex, they would be four times more elusive when being pursued."

~ **Bruce Bryans**

Introduction

When it comes to finding a suitable mate for a passion filled, committed relationship, one of the most important things men desire in a woman is self-possession, or said another way, womanly poise. When high-quality men come across a woman with poise, they not only feel a strong desire to be around her, but they also crave her respect and even her approval. These men love being in the company of a woman with poise. But even more so, they want to love and "possess" the woman who owns it.

Women of poise are rare and thus, highly sought after by men who exude masculine maturity. Why? It's because men like this understand that a woman's poise reflects her self-worth. These men understand that a woman can only act with poise when she's placed a higher importance on her dignity and well-being than she does ANY man. It is this unique female attitude that drives men wild with **sustainable desire**, the kind of desire that makes them eager to commit to a woman and claim her as their own.

Women without poise simply don't respect themselves enough. Don't get me wrong, they *do* have some level of self-respect, but it usually gets tossed out the window the moment a highly desirable male specimen takes a romantic interest in them. Women without poise generally give too much of themselves, and usually at the most ineffective times when dating a man. They are usually very lenient with men in the beginning stages of a new romance, and they're prone to compromising their standards just to keep a man in their life.

What's worse is that women without poise unknowingly chase men, as they become frantic, frustrated, and foolhardy whenever the guy they want begins to pull away or suddenly loses interest in them. A woman with poise never throws herself at a man this way nor does she make things easy for him by clearing her schedule "just in case" he calls or comes around. No. Instead, a woman with poise maintains her mystery, sticks to her standards, and uses her feminine charms to *invite* men to either pursue her passionately or simply leave her alone.

Poise and the High-Value Woman

The way you handle a man's good behavior; his thoughtfulness, affections, sacrifices, appreciation, gentleness, etc., AND the way you handle his not so good behavior; his thoughtlessness, presumptuousness, insults, and loss of interest means EVERYTHING to how he will perceive your self-worth. It's easy to illustrate class and character when things are going your way with a guy. But your ability to remain unfazed amid his disrespect, disinterest, disdain, or disregard is what really helps him determine whether you are a high-value woman or not.

You must accept that no matter how prepared you *think* you are, a man will not always act in ways that are favorable to you. Sometimes he may act presumptuously and try to make sexual advances on you that go beyond your level of comfort. Sometimes he may ask favors of you that make you feel as if you're being used. Sometimes he may simply say things to you in jest, not realizing that each time he does it insults your very soul. Sure, some men are scumbags and scallywags, but not all men who act thoughtlessly towards you should be categorized as such. Therefore, it's best to act with poise when it comes to men and dating so that you can separate the trash from the treasure.

When a scumbag or player meets a woman with poise, he'll realize he's wasting his time on her and will subsequently lose interest. When Mr. Right meets a woman with poise, he'll realize that *you're* not wasting your time and he'll do whatever he can to match your level of class. Your womanly poise is your power. Thus, your habitual responses to embarrassing dating situations, thoughtless male behavior, or unexpected mishaps on the road of love will tell a man if you are a woman of poise or a woman of powerlessness.

Dating Rules for the "Nice Girl"

This book was written for women who want to go from being powerless to possessing irresistible poise in how they date and relate with men. Because of this, it's best to think of this book as meant for "medicinal" purposes, meaning it will serve you best if you have trouble keeping men interested long enough to get a commitment. But as with all things, be careful of becoming an extremist, especially with seduction type advice that can immensely ramp up a man's attraction to you. Over doing it can create a whole new set of problems if you're not careful.

The women who will get the most out of this book are the ones who have a very specific problem, namely, that great guys seem to pull away, disappear, or lose interest before committing or even shortly after a relationship has developed. Hence, as a "medicinal" book, it is meant to "heal" a very specific issue, and it WILL work for you.

So, think of the concepts in this book as powerful *guidelines* to help you get the man you want as opposed to ironclad dating rules to which one must adhere. In fact, look at it this way: The more trouble you have keeping men interested in you long enough to get a commitment, the more you should stick to the guidelines within this book.

Now, I'm going to assume that you are the sweet kind of girl who already knows how to cultivate lovingness, comfort, and thus, convenience for a man. This book doesn't focus on that type of advice. In fact, I've already written two books to help women in this area, namely, *The 7 Irresistible Qualities Men Want In A Woman* and *Make Him BEG For Your Attention*. This book, however, will show you how to cultivate long-term attraction with a man by helping you to define and uphold your standards and personal boundaries. These are the very same standards and boundaries that help to inform a man of your high self-worth, and thus, your high-value as a potential long-term partner. So, because this book was designed specifically for the "Nice Girl" who's probably already very skilled at cultivating emotional comfort with a man (through her lovingness and tenderness), you won't find much advice of this nature.

The reason why I chose specifically not to focus on the more "loving" and "tender" behaviors is simply because this book was meant to help women who lean too much on the side of being excessively "nice" to the men they date. Don't get me wrong; feminine "niceness" is a highly desirable trait in a long-term romantic partner. However, as with anything in life, niceness can be taken to an extreme and thus only ends up communicating low self-worth. And this is a very common problem I see with many women of today and their approach to dating.

The thing is, being nice **at the expense of your standards and boundaries** causes men to see you (and treat you) like a doormat, which results in a major loss of attraction. This is one of the main reasons why men pull away, suddenly lose interest, and disappear in the beginning stages of a new romance. You can be as loving and as tender as a mother with her newborn, but being excessively nice at the expense of your standards and boundaries WILL cause men, even the most well-intentioned men, to lose their respect, and thus, their desire for you. Desire cannot be negotiated, and no amount of "niceness" can coerce a man to stick around if you cannot arouse and sustain his passion.

Remember, it is impossible for a man to fall in love and stay in love with a woman if he doesn't already respect her. Impossible. Men commit to women they perceive as "high-value" romantic partners. And this "high-value" is most clearly communicated to men through the way you *allow* them to treat you. Your acceptance and appraisal of a man's behavior towards you is the single most defining quality that informs him of your "worth" as a long-term romantic partner. Read that last sentence again.

So, as you read through this book, let's try to keep in mind that every single point within is meant to help you achieve two VERY specific things within the first few weeks and following months of a new romance:

1. These dating rules will help you intensify the emotional attraction of <u>men who are most likely to ask you for a commitment.</u>

2. These dating rules will help you to effectively weed out players, time wasters, deadbeats, and other unsuitable/low-interest suitors.

If attaining these two results sounds interesting to you, let's move forward shall we?

The Women That Need This Book

We've already defined the problem and the solution this book provides for that problem, but we still need to properly define the kind of woman I truly want to help with this book. I write all of my books with a particular woman in mind; those with sincere hearts, lots of love and respect to give, and who have a deep desire to find a high-quality, commitment-ready man to build a life with. I do this to ensure that the advice I give pertaining to how men think is not abused or misused by women.

With all that said, here are two ways to know if this book will benefit you or not:

1. You want to attract and keep the attention of a high-quality man (a man with high self-esteem, ambition, leadership qualities, compassion, cherishes commitment, has high-standards for himself, defends his personal boundaries, knows what he wants, speaks his mind, understands the value of relationships, and exudes masculine, sexual confidence).

2. You want to pursue and nurture a *loving relationship that can lead to marriage* with such a man.

If you're not interested in guys that will hold you to a high but reasonable standard (meaning he won't tolerate flaky or disrespectful behavior) or if you're not interested in cultivating a serious relationship with a masculine man who wants and values commitment...this book is not for you. If you want to attract one-night stands, so called "players", or forty something year-old bad boys who think commitment is just another curse word...this book is not for you.

To attract and keep the attention of a high-quality man from the beginning of a blossoming romance, you must successfully communicate your high-value to him by maintaining your sense of dignity and self-respect whether things are going *really* well or *really* terrible. If you **unknowingly** trade in your dignity and self-respect for a man's love, it will make him perceive you as being a doormat. Don't let a man perceive you as being a doormat. Doormat women do not arouse a man's devotion, and thus, they end up in dead-end relationships more often than not. This is the fate of the overly "Nice Girl."

This book will help you avoid this fate by revealing the dating habits, beliefs, and attitudes of the high-value woman; the very woman who remains loyal to her dating standards and personal boundaries **regardless of the status, desirableness, or "dreaminess" of the man she's dating**. So, if you're ready to hook Mr. Right from the first few weeks of dating so that he craves your closeness, longs for your companionship, and begs you for a commitment, I encourage you to read on.

**Chapter One:**

How to Date a Man to Get His Love

and Respect

1

**Know your standards and in what way
you expect to be treated by men; but be
sure that your demeanor is clearly
deserving of the treatment you desire.**

Contrary to popular belief, men aren't stupid. We
will treat a woman exactly the way she allows us to.
Why? Because we're designed to honor a woman's
wishes based on her genuine merit, and not her imagined
self-worth. You can beg, plead, cry, cajole, and even nag
us until the end of time to treat you a certain way, but if
your demands fail to match up to your actions, we're not
going to change. It's as simple as that.

What's even worse is if a man realizes that his subpar
behavior actually sparks your attraction and makes you
want him even MORE. If he realizes this, he will ignore
everything you say regarding your "dissatisfaction" with
the way he treats you. Don't train a man to treat you
poorly by showing him greater fondness whenever he
acts poorly.

This is why it is vitally important for a woman to be
fully aware of what she's attracted to and also what she
will and will not stand for WAY before she begins dating
a man. You should be well acquainted with your
boundaries and limitations and know exactly what
behaviors you will and will not tolerate from a potential
suitor before he takes a romantic interest in you. Without

a clear set of standards, you're leaving yourself open to "interpretations of the law" that, in the heat of the moment, can be easily surmounted by men who are particularly experienced in the art of seducing women and wasting their time.

If you're not clear on your rules of engagement, you're more likely to make allowances for a man to avoid turning him off. In fact, the *more* you like him the *more* you're likely to tone down your expectations of him. In situations like this it should actually be the other way around. The more you like a guy, the more steadfast you should be regarding your boundaries so as to ensure you don't make excuses for him because of his handsomeness, charm, wealth, social status, ethnicity, etc.

Women very often make excuses for men's behavior, especially in the beginning stages of a new romance; which is actually the worst time to be overly lenient with someone you barely know. For instance, it's one thing to accept last minute date plans with your long-term boyfriend, but it's imprudent to accept it from a guy who barely knows you. Why? Well, it's simply because he *barely knows you.* Hence, if you start things off with him by being overly lenient, you end up setting the foundation for future low-quality behavior.

Remember, you're not being demanding by having reasonable expectations for the men who take an interest in you. When a man finds you attractive enough to ask you out, you should assume this means he's interested in you and wants to "win" your approval just as much as you'd like to attain his. You're not being unreasonable by expecting him to contact you ahead of time with concrete plans, you're simply *assuming* he likes and respects you enough to put his best foot forward as he makes a serious attempt to win your admiration.

If you accept a last minute, half-thought out first date, he will expect you to accept a second one just as last minute and half-baked. He'll also expect a third one, and not surprisingly, a fourth one as well. Unless you graciously express your disappointment AND deny him your company at some point early on, don't expect him to act any differently. Your desire to be treated with forethought will be constantly denied so long as you remain unclear about what you expect from a man.

2

Be open to meeting and dating other men until a man has offered you exclusivity. While you should not hide the fact that you are dating other men, you should seek to reveal this information in a way that cultivates his curiosity.

Sometimes fate may have it where you're in a season of being so darn irresistible that men just can't seem to leave you alone. Good for you! What's even better is that in this season you might actually find yourself dating two or three potential Mr. Rights all at once. Just keep in mind that if you do find yourself in this situation or one like it, ensure that you're honest and upfront about it with the men involved early on. Whatever you do, don't lie about it just because you think you'll lose a guy's interest. Or worse, don't exaggerate the truth thinking it will make him want you more.

So, let's say you're casually dating two men at once. One is a handsome, charismatic chef with tons of ambition and the other is a steely, stoic carpenter who loves dogs. Let's say you've been out with both gentlemen a few times and each guy is fully aware that you're still "on the market" and dating other men. Over time, if neither guy makes an effort to become a central figure in your life, you can either continue casually dating them both or move on completely so that you can make room for more insistent suitors.

However, let's say Mr. Carpenter starts pursuing you more passionately, giving you more of his time and attention. If this happens, it's important that you reciprocate his ardor, but maintain your reluctance to be his and his alone. Just because he's taken greater interest in you doesn't mean you should immediately take yourself off the market. Don't jump the gun and *immediately* assume Mr. Carpenter wants an exclusive relationship with you based merely on his initial displays of interest. Remember, you're confident not desperate, and you need time to figure out if Mr. Carpenter really wants to be with you and only you.

So instead of getting overly eager and taking yourself off the market, continue dating both men casually while obviously giving more consideration to Mr. Carpenter. But **in time**, as things between you and Mr. Carpenter get serious, you should either:

1. Cease seeing our handsome chef and **coquettishly** inform Mr. Carpenter that presently, he's the only man in your life, or…

2. Simply wait for Mr. Carpenter to openly ask you

for an exclusive relationship.

The former option might be preferable if you find yourself no longer able to entertain both men casually. It might also be a better option if you know Mr. Carpenter is particularly high-status and more experienced with women. Why? Well, a high-quality man who's a bit more familiar with the dating game might want to be assured of your interest in and loyalty to him *before* offering you a commitment. If he's particularly confident, he might have been waiting for you to abandon the other casuals in your life as a test to see if you're as into him as he is in you.

Therefore, if you realize Mr. Carpenter has become more curious about the other men in your life, **assuming he's made it clear that he sees and/or wants a future with you**, it might be time for you to take a chance on him. If he's clearly proven both his sincerity and his reliability through his pursuit of you, it might be a good idea to show him your devotion by getting rid of Mr. Chef and any other doting stragglers in your life.

Now, the latter option might be a better idea if you're not exactly convinced of Mr. Carpenter's interest in you. Even if he's really into you, if he insists on playing it cool or being romantically timid, then you have every right to continue dating other men casually to find Mr. Right. Waiting for a man to offer you exclusivity before disregarding other suitors is always a better option when the guy you really want to be with appears undecided about you. Remember, the level of importance you give to a man should be closely proportionate to the consistency of his interest. If his interest in you seems ambiguous and cloudy, he should *not* be a major factor in your mind.

3

To avoid inadvertently disenchanting the man you desire, let your real-life interactions seize his longing before you attempt to befriend him on Facebook. It is to a woman's advantage to let a man establish an offline relationship with her before she initiates an online one with him.

If a guy hasn't made a "move" on you yet, meaning he hasn't gotten your phone number or asked you out on a date, etc., you should not add him on Facebook. Sure, you can *accept* his friend request if you find him attractive and interesting, but you should resist the temptation to <u>initiate</u> the 'friending' on Facebook.

This rule stands even if a guy gives you tons of attention at work, flirts with you more than anyone else, or pulls your hair every time you walk past him. Don't initiate an online relationship with him. You should never *assume* a man is romantically interested in you *until* he proves otherwise through his attempts to get to know you outside of work, school, recreational functions, or wherever it is you keep "bumping" into him.

A man can learn a lot about a woman simply by observing her Facebook profile. A lot. And if you haven't been particularly vigilant in curating your profile page, there are probably some bizarre pages you "liked", immature posts, and unbecoming photos (you know the ones) that could compel a guy to form an unfair, although understandable, opinion about you.

Online communities like Facebook in particular, while they glamourize the great things about our lives, they also exaggerate the unflattering and undignified things about us as well. This is why giving a guy, one who doesn't know the real you yet, immediate access to your online world might cause him to arrive at unfair conclusions about you; as these unfair conclusions will be based mainly on the visual story that your profile reveals to him.

Your immortalized adventures, such as *Jeanette's College Mardis Gras Unleashed Vol. 2* or *Jeanette's Visual Journal of Ex-Boyfriends*, if left un-curated, have the potential to turn relationship-minded men off of you before they even get a chance to ask you out. Sure, all those bizarre pages you "liked", immature posts, and unbecoming photos aren't wholly representative of the mature, elegant, self-possessed woman you are today, but *he* doesn't know that yet. Thus, giving him access to your online world before he's had an opportunity to be captivated by the real, present-day you could cause a potential Mr. Right to suddenly lose interest.

The best time to initiate any kind of online connection with a man (such as Facebook friending) is *after* HE gets the ball rolling. If you've already been out with him several times and you're really digging him, it's okay to add him first. If he's gotten your phone contact and has been consistent and persistent in keeping in touch with you, again, it's okay to add him first.

It is okay to friend request him in these situations because he's already made his romantic interest in you clear. In fact, initiating the Facebook relationship at this point is a great way to let him know that you're very interested in him as well. It makes it clear that you appreciate his attention and that you want to expand the breadth of your connection with him. And the fact that you *waited* awhile to add him will make him value your friend request even more.

When a man is looking for a woman with long-term relationship or marriage potential, one of the ways he appraises her value is by how easy or difficult it is to access her intimacies. While these obviously include a woman's physical intimacies, men are also concerned with a woman's social intimacies as well, especially if he might be open to a committed relationship with her. Thus, not giving a guy immediate access to your online world makes him perceive you as being *high-value*, which, in his eyes, immediately separates you from other women.

This is especially the case if the guy you're interested in is quite the catch. If he's a highly desirable and sought-after male specimen, he might be quite accustomed to having random, interested women add him on Facebook with little to any effort on his part. This is why one of the simplest yet effective things you can do to avoid being seen as "basic", "commonplace", or "meh" in the eyes of a man is to simply wait for him to make a move (or several moves) on you *before* you make him a part of your online world.

4

When a man asks you out on a first date, it is acceptable to let him pay for said date. However, be sure to graciously display and voice your willingness to "split the bill" with him if he so desires.

If a guy asks you out on a date you should assume that he is paying for said date. This should be your expectation. There's nothing wrong with thinking this way, as most men have accepted this as being part of their role in the dating process. In general, we don't have a problem picking up the cheque if we've invited you to spend some one-on-one time with us.

Now, even though there's nothing wrong with expecting the man who asked you out to foot the bill, you should be careful not to develop an entitled attitude. I've come across some toxic dating advice that encourages women to go on as much fully paid first, second, and third dates with men as possible, even if they know from the first date that they're not really that interested in these men. This kind of advice, along with a culture that tends to over-romanticize the "independent woman", has caused some women to adopt a self-entitled, unappreciative, and unsympathetic attitude towards the sacrifices men make (and *want* to make) to incite their romantic interest. Because of this, men now *expect* the women they date to either pay their own way or hint at their willingness to do so.

To help ease the awkwardness of first date expectations between the sexes, women are encouraged to do the "courtesy reach" when the bill arrives. This occurs when a woman reaches for her purse to pay her share, at which point the man will graciously refuse her offer and insist on paying for everything himself. The problem with relying on the "courtesy reach" alone is that more and more men are becoming privy to it, which makes it somewhat less special when a woman actually does it.

Initially, the "courtesy reach" was supposed to be a way for a woman to display both her progressive approach to dating and genuine kindness towards her gentleman love interest. By reaching for her purse, to a man it would appear as if she's not looking for a free ride at his expense. The gesture is meant to make a man believe that a woman who does the courtesy reach is both highly considerate and generous, which thus makes her superior to her peers.

These days, however, because men have become quite accustomed to the "courtesy reach", it will only separate a woman from her peers up to a certain extent. Therefore, if you really want to communicate your kindness, generosity, and high-value to a man, you might benefit more by taking it a step further. Instead of quietly reaching for your purse, letting a man reject your offer, and graciously obliging him, you should actually *tell him* that you are willing to pay for your share. Let him actually *hear you* offer to pay your share, then let him lead from there. If he relinquishes and allows you to pay, so be it. If he politely rejects your offer and insists that he pays, so be it. Just remember to graciously express your appreciation for his gentlemanly offer with a sincere 'thank you.'

Remember, you must allow a man to reveal himself to you through his leadership (or lack thereof). By going a step beyond the "courtesy reach" you'll place yourself in a rare and highly attractive category of women – those who do not take a man's company for granted and are genuinely interested in contributing.

Of course, first date "rules" such as these can change depending on your situation. For one, if you're a woman in your early twenties, the guys in your age bracket might not be in a financial position to pay your way. Guys in their early twenties are usually either in college or trying to establish themselves in their work and careers. Men in this age bracket are also a little less experienced when it comes to properly courting a woman. Hence, you may find yourself disappointed if your twenty-two-year-old crush asks you out and awkwardly waits for you to pull out your purse and offer to go Dutch.

I'm of the opinion that the older the gentleman, the more refined he *should* be when it comes to courting a woman. A forty-something year old man who's brazen enough to ask you out should feel honored to pay for the date, especially if you were an absolute delight to be with. There's nothing wrong with expecting a man to act his age, especially when it comes to the traditionally accepted cultural mores of first date etiquette.

If you want to screen the men you date for quality, allow them to reveal their **maturity** regarding how they woo you. On a first date, you must expect (not insist) guys to treat you with honor and propriety. There's no reason why a forty-something year old man should be dating you like a twenty-two-year-old college crush. You might find it funny if your college sophomore crush awkwardly clears his throat and glances at your purse when the bill arrives, but it's not as cute if your forty-something year old new love interest does the exact same thing.

5

Be judicious when it comes to 'last minute dates.' Consistently accepting last minute dates is a lousy way to begin and sustain a relationship.

During the beginning stages of a new romance, you should expect a man to make a <u>clear</u> effort to capture your attention and impress you. So, while there's nothing inherently wrong with accepting a man's last-minute plans for a spontaneous date, keep in mind that this sort of spontaneity is best reserved for a relationship in which a reasonable level of *consistency* already exists. This is where many women make mistakes when it comes to Mr. Spontaneous-Dates. They confuse "spontaneity" with "romantic laziness" and instead of refusing last minute dates early on they accept them, and thus set the trend for a very subpar (and ultimately disappointing) romantic experience.

I know this point will be difficult for some women to accept, especially since last minute texts to meet up and hang out seems to define modern dating. But if a man is romantically interested in you, he should at least try to put some forethought into his wooing efforts. Last minute texts to "meet up", "do something", "have some fun", or "hang out" might have been cute in college, but at this stage in your adult life you should feel amused if not slightly miffed whenever a guy hits you up with last minute plans for a first or second date.

The thing is, if a man is smitten enough to ask you out he will rise to meet your expectations, especially if he thinks you're a high-value woman. Accepting last minute dates early on quickly removes the veil of "high-value" he might have already given you. As is the nature of all human beings, men will naturally take the path of least resistance to get what they want. Thus, by accepting his last-minute date requests in the beginning, you give him consent to continue pursuing you with as little effort possible.

Remember, as men, we value that which we have worked and sacrificed for in order to attain. Hence, setting a high but reasonable standard regarding those first few dates could be the game changer you need to make men take you more seriously. This is especially true if the guys you date don't seem to stick around longer than a few short weeks.

Now, don't worry about guys who label you as "high-maintenance" or "inflexible" just because you politely refuse their spontaneous date request. They're either insane, self-entitled, or both. If a man immediately loses interest in you because you declined a last-minute date, consider yourself lucky. Chances are he was probably more interested in getting his way with you than cultivating a relationship.

Of course, once a guy has proven himself to be *reliable* in taking the initiative to plan dates, you can be a little more lenient in terms of any last-minute plans.

Let's say you've already been out on three or four well-planned dates with him where you both had a ton of fun and seemed to have great chemistry. If he calls you on the very night of some fun event and wants to pick you up within the hour to go out with him, assuming you're not busy with something else, take him up on his offer. At this point, it's okay to accept and even expect a bit more dating spontaneity because he's already proven to you that he values your attention and respects your time.

My only caveat is to ensure that the spontaneous dates don't begin to outnumber the planned ones. No man is perfect, and it's ridiculously easy to fall into bad habits (we've all been guilty of it). Therefore, if you begin noticing that your new beau rarely plans things out anymore, simply give him the benefit of the doubt and graciously ask him to give you a little more heads up in the future. If he really wants you and cares about your dignity, he's more likely to honor your boundaries. But if your polite suggestion doesn't work, you're free to resort to Plan B: Respectfully refuse his last-minute offers and suggest another time.

6

Do not accept dates in which you must travel too far from your home surroundings, especially in the beginning of a new romance. A good man will be concerned about your comfort and safety, and will therefore ensure that the venues

chosen for a date are within a reasonable distance to your home.

While there might be a handful of very, very, (very) unique situations that would make it "okay" for a woman to travel a bit far from her home environment to date a guy, for the most part, this is a bad idea. When a woman is too eager and willing to take on the burden of a time-consuming commute just to date a guy, it tells a man that she's already given him a higher place of importance in her mind than she holds in his own. And once this occurs, the power dynamic eventually shifts from him pursuing you to him expecting to be habitually pursued *by you*.

Sometimes men will either consciously or subconsciously test a woman just to see how willing she is to please him. While I always encourage women to work their seductive magic so that they can be *pleasing* to a man, I insistently discourage them from falling into the trap of trying too hard to *please* them. A woman is pleasing to a man when she allows her grace and femininity to permeate her appearance, personality, and demeanor. A woman falls into pleasing a man when, because of her niceness, desperation, or inexperience, she is overly willing and eager to acclimate herself into his lifestyle.

While there's nothing fundamentally wrong with going out of your way to meet your alleged Mr. Right for a date, habitually doing so inhibits his ability to sustain long-term attraction to you. From his point of view, your willingness to take on the burden of a long commute or an inconvenient rendezvous immediately lowers your status while increasing his own.

But why does this happen?

It all has to do with the nature of men and how we're hard-wired to fall in love with a woman.

You see, to capture a man's heart you must appeal to his chivalry, i.e. – his romantic side. Taking on a time-consuming commute or meeting him at venues that clearly take you way beyond the comfort zone of your "home environment" will kill his desire for chivalry. What's worse is that if he's prone to player-like tendencies, it will cause him to see you as a short-term love interest. To be *pleasing* to a man without trying to *please* him in this way is to see yourself as being something *precious*. Seeing yourself as being precious and worthy of being wooed within the confinements of your comfort zone is the feminine element that men are secretly attracted to in women. Men secretly want to *feel* the emotions of a great romantic conquest. Unfortunately, it is difficult for a man to feel such emotion if a woman agrees to (or worse, commits herself to) a long commute for dates.

When a man insists that a woman must not take on unnecessary expenses or encumbrances just to spend time with him, it is the mark of a true gentleman. This is a man who is concerned about your comfort, safety, and ultimately, your wellbeing, the kind of man who is determined to cultivate both your romantic attraction to him as well as the emotional comfort you feel towards him. Men who only want you for the moment (or maybe a few moments) will focus solely on cultivating romantic attraction with little to no regard for your emotional comfort. Thus, when a man thinks very highly of a woman, he is less likely to exploit her natural desire to acclimatize herself to his lifestyle. Read that last sentence again.

Travelling too far from your home environment to date a guy is not a good idea if you want to easily separate the men who only want you for the moment from those who might want you for a lifetime. You must keep in mind that women are naturally hard-wired to create comfort and *convenience* for men. They are far more accommodating by the nature of their gender, and thus, it's much easier for a woman to slip into cultivating comfort at the expense of long-term attraction.

Basically speaking, any sort of dating behavior that makes things "too easy" for a man early on will prove detrimental to your ability to sustain long-term attraction. Until some sort of consistent relationship (i.e. – commitment) has been established, you shouldn't be taxing your own time and resources just to spend time with a man.

Now, I know for a fact that this advice will be difficult for many women to stomach. I'd even wager that the older a woman is the more willing she is to go out of her way to accommodate the men she dates by going the distance to meet up with them, even if it is at her expense. Don't do this. No matter how independent or progressive you may think it is to meet your Mr. McDreamy on his turf sometimes, you must learn to separate how you *wish* men were from how men really think. And quite frankly, few things make a man romantically lazy (and thus, entitled) faster than a woman who is willing to go through hell and high water just to meet up with him.

Remember, until a man has already established you as being a high-value woman who is worth his love and loyalty, you must not make it *easier* for him to spend time with you. If you live two hours away from him, that is HIS burden to bear, not yours. And it goes without saying that if he lives a city, county, state, or continent away from you, this is also HIS burden to bear, not yours. Let him figure out the logistics for himself, as he'll be more likely to place a higher value on your attention if he's the one taking on most of the burdens to see you. Allow him the freedom to remove the obstacles to your love that are **already in his way**. If a man is really determined to have you in his life, he'll navigate hell and high water to wedge his way into yours.

In the beginning of a new romance, don't let a man's high status, economic success, future promises, charm, attractiveness, or sad stories seduce you into navigating hell and high water just to spend time with him. If you live a good distance away from each other and he is still determined to spend time with you, do not deprive him of this burden. Yes, you will lose out on some men (the time wasters) by maintaining this standard, but you'll also make yourself immensely attractive to the kinds of men (the chivalrous) who would cross the Pacific a thousand times to secure your love.

7

Unless it is a one-off emergency and your Prince Charming is most certainly out of options, you do not acquiesce when a man asks you for money or makes inappropriate requests of your resources.

So as not to insult your intelligence, I am going to keep this insanely short: If you want to avoid feeling used and getting played, you would be wise not to entertain or encourage the attention of men who are brazen enough to ask you for money, who demand access to your resources/connections, or who attempt to cajole you into performing time-intensive favors for them. No self-respecting man is going to ask a woman he's romantically interested in for money, unless it's a dire emergency, he's forgotten his wallet, and he couldn't get in contact with friends and family fast enough to resolve the situation. And no romantically sincere gentleman is going to try to get something from you just because you have insider access or special connections.

Regarding money in particular, I cannot think of any reason other than an immediate emergency in which a man would or should ask for your assistance. I mean, even *if* it is an emergency and the gentleman in question is forced to ask you for money, please ensure that it's an amount you can immediately spare and that he's very embarrassed and insistent that you'll be paid back.

If it seems like I'm being harsh, it's because I am. I have a daughter, and when she reaches the age where she'll be dating to find a man worth her love and loyalty I will tell her the exact same thing. High-quality men with immense levels of self-respect would rather chew off their own arm than ask a potential love interest for her money, her time-intensive/resource-consuming favors, or access to her connections.

Of course, like I said in the beginning of this point, there will be rare and unique situations where this might happen and where a gentleman is forced to ask for a helping hand. Life happens, and sometimes a lifelong romance can be sparked out of some of the most

28

embarrassing and untimely situations. However, these are the exceptions, not the rule.

For example, on a particularly great third date with a phenomenal young lady, something super embarrassing (embarrassing to me at least) occurred. It was night time, and at the end of our date, no matter how much I pleaded, rain-danced, or offered up prayers and burnt offerings, my car refused to start. Apparently, my car battery had unceremoniously died on me without so much as a cordial farewell. Without complaint, my date drove home (it was a five-minute drive) and came back fifteen minutes later with battery jumper cables in the dead of night to help me bring my car back to life. About a year and half later, I married her.

Now, I presented that little story not to motivate you to give men money, favors, and resources whenever they're in a bind. I told you this story to illustrate how an embarrassing situation for a man might actually be an opportunity for you to display your resourcefulness, helpfulness, and positive attitude in the midst of his distress. As with every other point in this book, treat this "rule" more like a guideline and use your common sense and female intuition to direct your decisions.

Even if they are in dire straits at the moment, most men won't ask you for money, favors, or resources, especially if you're not their girlfriend yet. But if you find yourself in a **very unique situation** with great guy who is out of options (and jumper cables), don't be too quick to leave him to his fate or at the mercy of the elements. If you genuinely get a sense that his situation is just one of those unforeseen "plights of life" moments, help him out. It could very well be a defining moment for the relationship. However, if you get a nauseating feeling in your gut that a man is trying to capitalize on your kindness or take advantage of you in some way, you should trust your gut, leave him where he stands, and don't look back.

8

Like all virtues, "amicableness", though a highly desirable trait in a woman, can be taken to an extreme. Never allow your desire for a man to stifle your authenticity. You will gain his respect and adoration when you *do not* agree with him about things in which you genuinely don't approve.

When it comes to first impressions, the more warm, cordial, and friendly you are, the more likely your Prince Charming will to see you as long-term relationship material. When a man is looking for a potential girlfriend, within those first few dates he will be very observant of your behavior to find out if you possess a congenial and easy-going personality. However, although your initial success with men is highly dependent on your amicability, you should never feign agreeableness towards things that you genuinely don't agree with, like, or support.

Being overly agreeable with him about everything won't make you seem like a dream-girl. Instead, to him, it will make you seem like a doormat...a doormat that

ANY man, not just him, can walk on and use. No man, especially a high-quality man, wants a committed relationship with a doormat that any man can walk on and use.

If you're especially prone to being overly nice (especially towards men you consider "out-of-your-league"), in your mind you might think that not speaking up about certain things or agreeing with him will make him like you even more. You might even think that concealing your opinions or ignoring your feelings about something will make him want to see more of you.

Don't be misled.

Being too acquiescent with men conceals your authenticity, which thus makes it near impossible for us to experience and fall in love with the real you. Therefore, you should not alter your likes, dislikes, preferences, tastes, and standards just to keep a man interested in you. Maintain the self-belief that your ideal Mr. Right won't disappear the moment you disapprove of something he does or disagree with him about something. The man who wants an equal partner will value your honesty, even if that honesty makes him feel momentary discomfort or unease.

Seriously, think about it for a moment.

If you're casually dating a guy who isn't emotionally mature enough to simply "agree to disagree" with you, how much success do you think you'll have in a relationship with him? Concealing your authenticity might make him believe you're a good match for him, but once a serious relationship develops he'll either become disenchanted when he gets a taste of the real you or he'll simply lose interest from being bored with your blandness. Hence, being **gracefully honest** with your

31

likes and dislikes early on is a great way to weed out incompatible men as well as guys who are only looking for an easy-ride at your expense.

Like every other point in this book, this piece of advice is all about finding the healthy middle ground between maintaining your standards while trying to cultivate emotional closeness with a man. You don't have to go towards the other extreme and become an ice-cold harpy if a man does or says something of which you don't approve. And you don't have to become hyper antagonistic if you don't share his views on a particular topic. Graciousness, poise, and refinement of speech will make it far easier for the right man to relate with you even if he doesn't agree with you. So, remember to always keep it classy when you disagree with him or when you feel compelled to express your disapproval.

9

The masterful seducer will use sympathetic language, passive-aggressive rhetoric, and reality-distorting diction to make you believe in him. If you find your heart being softened and swayed to act in a man's favor, despite feeling anxious and confused, CLING to your boundaries.

There will be some situations with men in which it will be in your best interest to ignore your emotions, steel your mind, and cling to your boundaries. These are the situations where you may either be dealing with a wolf in sheep's clothing or a relatively good guy who *thinks* he knows what's best for the relationship. A wolf in sheep's clothing is simply a man who's hoping to capitalize on your feminine sympathies. On the other hand, the good guy who thinks he knows what's best is just a man whose self-interest is being powered by his hormones.

Falling for a man's persistence and earnestness can sometimes lead your heart astray if you haven't fully developed a built-in lie detector. Even if you are very familiar with the games men play, you might still find yourself up against an opponent who, because of his seductive prowess or high-desirability, can tap into the deep reservoirs of kindness in your heart for his own benefit.

The key to overcoming those confusing and often challenging situations is to cling to your boundaries in spite of how you *feel* at the moment. To do this successfully, you must become exceedingly comfortable telling him "NO" and you must also know what your standards are so that you don't have to conjure one up in the heat of the moment. For example, if you've already determined that you're not the kind of girl who drives too far away from home for a date, it's a lot easier to stick to this standard even if your dream guy begs you to do it "just for him."

Another example? Let's say you've already decided that a man who disappears and reappears in and out of your life more than twice is dead to you. If he disappears then reappears a third time, unannounced, and this time with two tickets to that thing you like, what do you do? Of course, as a high-value woman you might tell him

"Thanks, but no thanks. I'm busy. And I'm guessing you're often busy as well since you can't seem to keep in touch with me." But what if he begins telling you how expensive the tickets are, how this is a once in a lifetime event, and how he's been wanting to take you to this special event from since you first told him how much you love it. What if he tells you that he hasn't been keeping in touch because his dog was sick, his goldfish died, his car was stolen, or some other sad and thoroughly convincing story? What do you do then?

Things could get a little confusing if every fiber of your being has already told you that this guy is a waste of time, and now all of a sudden, those very same fibers are starting to reconsider. Once your "super-nice, super-sweet, super-accommodating" heartstrings have been plucked, you'll find yourself coming up with strong reasons why you should ignore his past behavior and just give him another chance. As you can see, you cannot trust "the fibers of your being" because their opinions change based on the latest information. And in cases like this, where a man's earnestness is not a good indicator of his integrity, you cannot trust your heart to decide either. A man can be totally earnest with you...but wrong. He can be exceedingly sincere and well-meaning...but tremendously incorrect all at the same time.

When a man is thoroughly convincing and confusing all at once, stick to your principles. If his earnestness, persistence, candor, and sacrifice arouse your self-doubt and sympathy rather than your confidence in him, stick to your principles.

As human beings, we would like to believe that we're rational creatures that make rational decisions more often than not. Unfortunately, the reality is that most of us make decisions based on our subconscious emotions and we rationalize those decisions only *after* they've already been made. This is why you should resist the temptation to rationalize away a man's mistakes for him. Don't allow men to use your sympathies to further their self-interest. If you have a high but reasonable relationship standard and the guy you're dating has already blown his chances, stick to your guns, embrace your self-confidence, and defer to your ideals. Your principles are unemotional, unbending, and unbiased. They will always lead you to clarity when a man selfishly attempts to sway your sympathies for his own benefit.

Chapter Two:

Power Dating Strategies for finding

Mr. Right

10

If you wish to sustain a man's interest longer than a few dates, you must create the impression that while you desire his closeness you also draw pleasure from your freedom. A man's desire to claim a woman as his own is greatly intensified when she appears cheerful in her independence yet eager for his intimacy.

If there is one thing that can drive a man crazy and make him BEG to see you again it is your ability to illustrate a cheerful independence and selective desire at the same time. In the beginning stages of a new romance, when the mystery is high and a man's interest is keen, nothing floods his brain with thoughts of being with you faster than a merry display of your independence mixed with a seductive display of your **discriminating** interest.

A display of cheerful independence is simply anything that shows that you actually have a life of your own and that you enjoy it. One of the things that quickly attracts a man's attention is a woman's joie de vivre or, her zest for life so to speak. When a woman is determined to get the most and make the most out of her life it speaks volumes about her character, personality, and thus, her self-respect. It makes her even *more* attractive when she does not give up her personal merriments (hobbies, friends, interests, pursuits, etc.) the moment a man takes an interest in her.

A display of discriminating interest is simply the way a woman communicates her desire for a man's closeness. As a man is getting to know you better and is becoming more and more interested in you, he wants to know that you are just as eager to get close to him as he is to you. Men require a sincere display of your romantic desire to inspire them to make the sacrifices necessary to pursue you for a commitment.

But more importantly, a man wants to know that your romantic desire is highly selective and very discriminating. On some level, every man wants to believe that his dream girl could have easily selected *other* men to be with, but that she had no choice but to place her attention on him because he was simply *better* than them. A seductive display of your discriminating interest will make him feel significant, and thus, make you appear highly selective; which is an extremely attractive trait in a woman.

What trips many women up is the apparent paradox of communicating their desirableness while also expressing their own sincere and highly selective desire for a man. In theory, it sounds confusing, but in practice it's actually quite simple to do.

The key to doing this successfully is to always be on the lookout for opportunities to <u>subtly hint</u> that:

1. You are a high-value woman because you have a fun, vibrant life of your own.

2. Other men are *possibly* on the scene and *might* be enjoying your company, and…

3. You are thinking about him and wish he were

enjoying life *with you.*

I should specify that your <u>subtle hints</u> should convey that you wish *he* were with *you,* and not the other way around. You see, telling a man *"I wish you were here with me"* has a very different emotional effect than saying *"I wish I was there with you."* The former implies that your life is already fun but would be even more delicious with his presence. The latter subconsciously hints that you don't have anything else better to do than pine for his company and hope he invites you along in the future. The former statement communicates your high-value and selective desire, while the latter hints that your happiness is at his mercy.

Remember, words have deeper implied meanings, whether we'd like to admit it or not. So choose your words carefully, because they can increase your status in a man's eyes just as easily as they can lower your status, and thus, your importance to a man.

But how does a girl communicate her high-value and selective desire in a practical, everyday way? Well, here's an example to get you started:

Let's say your new love interest calls you while you are already out with the girls and having a great time. I suggest you don't answer him if you're in the thick of the fun and simply wait until your spectacular night is over before getting back to him. When you do get the opportunity (either after settling in for the night or waiting for the following morning) text him with something like this:

- *"Hey Eric, sorry I missed your call. I was out with the girls. Had a great night of dancing. Too bad you weren't there to dance with me. ;)"*

Now, if you really can't resist picking up the phone when he calls (shame on you), simply give him a variation to the response above; something like this:

- *"Hey Eric, sorry I can't talk right now. I'm having a great time dancing with my friends. Really wish you were here to dance with me though."*

In these situations, you're communicating to Eric that you have a fun life (happiness), that you enjoy time with your friends (social proof), and that you were thinking about him specifically and want to see more of him (selective desire). Responding like this creates both *anxiety* and *eagerness* in Eric's mind. This is a GOOD thing, especially in the beginning of a new romance.

The *anxiety* Eric feels has to do with his own imagination, as he'll secretly conjure up thoughts about the guys that might be hitting on you, the guys you might be dancing with, and the guys who might steal your heart away before he has a chance to do so himself. If he's particularly masculine, this *anxiety* of male competition will spike his testosterone (thus increasing his desire to compete for you) and make him even more *eager* to wedge himself into your life as swiftly as possible.

(By the way, I'm REALLY giving you an inside look into the male psyche when it comes to what arouses us to pursue a woman. So be sure to read and RE-READ that last paragraph until the secrets sink in.)

Let's do another example.

Let's say your new love interest texts you to see what you have planned for the evening. If you're not out on the town yet but you do have plans to go out with your friends, perhaps a reply text like this might work:

41

- *"I'm going out with my friends tonight like we planned a while back. Really wished you could come with, but...it's 'girls' night.' ;) Maybe next weekend?"*

If you're feeling particularly flirty, you can send a tempting little follow up:

- *"By the way, here's what I'm wearing tonight..."*

Then attach a classy selfie of you in that gorgeous little black dress.

Any red-blooded man who receives a playful, inviting, and high-value text like that will message you back immediately with concrete plans to see you the following weekend (or perhaps even the following day if possible). And I'm sure I don't have to tell you just how much he'll be thinking about you the entire time you're out with your friends.

Being cheerfully independent while subtly expressing your desire for him in a teasing way will give him "butterflies" and make him feel as if he's in high school again. If he has a sincere interest in you, this sort of playfulness will ramp up the sexual tension (attraction) and make him think of all sorts of creative ways to spend more time with you.

So, memorize this equation and write it someplace where you can be reminded of it daily as you interact with men:

Cheerful Independence (I don't <u>need</u> you to have fun, be happy, and get my needs met) + **Selective Desire** (But I <u>want</u> you more than any other man I could have because I think you're better than them) = **Deep Attraction in Men**. Remember that.

11

Never postpone your life or clear your schedule in hopes that a new love interest will contact you or ask you out. Fill your empty schedule with interesting activities and social engagements so that your mind will not grow anxious in the absence of a man's attention.

You can tell a lot about a woman's level of self-respect based on what she does with her time away from a man during a blossoming romance. Does she postpone her life and clear her schedule after a great first or second date with a guy? Does she cancel weekend engagements with her friends and family after getting a vague text from a guy about meeting "sometime this weekend"? Does she Krazy glue her smartphone to her waist to ensure that Mr. McDreamy's call or text doesn't go missed? Does she keep a tab perpetually open on her Internet browser so that she can check her Facebook inbox in five-minute intervals (causing her to be less productive on the job)?

These are all questions you should consider because we've all been guilty of making it easy for a new love interest to squeeze their way in our lives. While there's nothing wrong with being hopeful and expectant that a guy is going to ask you out again or contact you, be careful that you aren't slowly turning yourself into an anxiety-riddled mess by over doing it. Keep your activities, honor your engagements, and resist making someone a priority before they've *proven* that they are worth your mental energy.

I know this is easier said than done, especially if you are more prone to anxious thinking and compulsive behaviors. If you know you've been weak in this area in the past, you will have to give yourself a little more tough love than the average girl. Be pre-emptive about your habit of getting overly excited and anxious about a new guy by going a bit overboard on the activities. Assuming you trust their judgments, call your closest girlfriends (or mom) and have them keep you accountable. Ask for overtime from your boss, or, if you're self-employed, take up a new side project to keep you busy. Take up charity work if you must, or fill up the time with family commitments, like offering to babysit your sister's five kids (may God have mercy on you). Again, this advice is specifically for women **who know for a fact** that they have a predisposition for clearing their schedules and postponing their lives for men.

Finally, though you must have a busy or at least, engaging schedule, always be *responsive* whenever your new love interest contacts you or asks to see you again. Men are VERY sensitive to a woman's responsiveness, especially when they're just getting to know her. In fact, a man doesn't mind being rebuffed or rejected by a woman so long as it appears that she is:

1. Appreciative of his attention, and...

2. Enthusiastic about seeing him in the future.

These two things are vitally important, as they are the elements that help men determine a woman's level of responsiveness.

So, if a guy contacts you at an inopportune moment, don't be afraid to tell him that you're happy to hear from him but that you'll contact him later when you get a free minute. If you want to ramp up the romantic tension and arouse his emotional desire, you might even want to playfully suggest that he's been on your mind "once or twice" since your last meeting. If your new guy asks you out for a Friday night date but you've already promised that time to someone (or something) else, graciously decline but suggest when you'll be free again. So, to reiterate: keep your mind busy, be warm and responsive to him, and let him figure out the best way to squeeze himself into your life.

12

Be aware of men who enjoy feeding their egos with your attention. When a man desires to keep you both interested and perpetually single, his communication with you will be both charming and intermittent. His messages are designed to fan the flames of your desire and to test the depths of your desperation to be with him. If you respond to these half-hearted communication attempts, he will have determined that you are, in fact, starved for attention, and thus, the kind of woman he can "lead on" indefinitely.

Are you familiar with the term "dangle the carrot"? It basically means to tempt someone or something towards a course of action by consistently offering them an **unobtainable** reward. If you have ever dated a guy who seems to disappear and reappear in and out of your life while using playful and cryptic text messages to "keep in touch", you can be sure you've been the unwary victim of his "dangle the carrot" strategy.

Some men are masters at "dangling the carrot" in front of women to keep them interested in them. The "carrot" in this case is a man's tender attention and boyish charm, and he takes full advantage of his smartphone or social media to create the illusion that he's still interested in you and wants to move things forward someday. This is the guy that will waste your time indefinitely, as he'll send you inconsistent, intermittent, and flirtatious texts or Facebook messages without ever really asking you out or making any noticeable progression towards dating you.

A guy's carrot dangling strategy is easy to spot if you are willing to get real with yourself. For example, if you've been texting a guy "on and off" for two months or more and he hasn't confirmed any plans to actually meet-up (or if he did make plans, they quickly fell through the cracks because he cancelled), he might be tempting you with the carrot.

Another example? Let's say you've been out on one or two dates with a guy and he hasn't asked you out again AND it's already been several weeks. If he consistently texts you out of the blue with charming Facebook messages, drunk "I miss you" texts, random "Hey, beautiful(s)", or flirty emoticons, chances are he's just checking up on you to ensure that he's still hot on your mind in some capacity. In situations like this, what he's actually doing is fishing for some attention to feed his ego and to confirm your ever-burning desire to "meet-up" or "hook-up" someday.

When (not if) you find yourself in these situations, ignore him. Whether he randomly hits you up through text or on Facebook doesn't matter. Even if he sends you a shirtless pic of himself, ignore him. Even if he texts you at three o'clock in the morning to say he "misses you" ...ignore him (he's probably drunk or had just been dumped anyway). Your best bet is to ignore messages from guys like this if you want to avoid feeding their egos and thus, wasting your time.

Entertaining men like this isn't just a waste of time because you'll never get the relationship you want. It's a waste of time because it will draw your attention away from the *other* men in your immediate environment that might actually want something real and substantial with you. If playing into a man's carrot dangling game feels fun, flirty, and laid back, it's because you actually *do* enjoy at least *some* of his attention (especially if you believe he's a "catch").

Nevertheless, don't be misled. Chasing his carrot is dangerous to your love life in the long-run because it tricks you into focusing your emotional energy into a dead investment. Don't focus your emotional energy into a dead investment. Respect yourself enough to completely ignore a man when he begins to dangle the carrot in front of you. The only thing men like this really want from you is your attention and easy access to your female pleasures as well.

13

As a man makes himself a central figure in your life and demonstrates an unwavering interest in you, show him that you have eyes for him and him alone.

Jonathan and Stacey have been casually dating for about a month and they both seem to be *very* interested in their new and blossoming relationship. Jonathan is what you might call an eligible bachelor and the "perfect gentleman."

His mother is a particularly pretty woman, one who attracts male attention naturally. Over the years Jonathan has watched her refuse, ignore, and outright reject other men (even men of greater success and social status than his father) without even thinking about it. This, along with his happy childhood has made him deeply respectful of his parents' relationship, as he knows that a strong, loving marriage helps to raise respectful, well-adjusted children.

Jonathan is at a stage in his life where he's looking for "The One" woman he can commit to for a lifetime. He wants someone honest, kind, warm, supportive, and as loyal as his mother. He wants to be with a woman whom he can completely trust and depend on, a woman who will have eyes for him and him alone.

Stacey is what you might call an exceptional beauty and can be somewhat of a flirt. She possesses an incredible charm and she has a natural way with people. She makes friends easily and people are quickly drawn to her. She has lots of friends and acquaintances, many of them men, men who are stuck in her "friend-zone." Because of her natural assets, she has never had any problems attracting men and relationships, but just like any other woman, *keeping* the men she really wanted has been quite the challenge. Unsurprisingly, the male attention she constantly receives (and often encourages) has cost her various relationships in the past. And only recently has Stacey "toned it down" so that she doesn't end up driving away another interested suitor.

You've probably realized by now that Stacey's natural charm and enjoyment of male attention will pose a stumbling block to her blossoming relationship with Jonathan. Because of Jonathan's relationship wants and needs, **he will be tuned in to any female behavior that either reinforces or weakens his long-term desire for Stacey**. Of course, nothing Stacey does will ever make her the "perfect" woman, but her interactions with Jonathan will eventually allow him to ascertain if she's at least "perfect" *for him*.

Now, you're probably thinking that Stacey's chances with Jonathan are pretty much screwed. You wouldn't be far from the truth in an average scenario, but because Stacey has decided to "tone it down" regarding her enthusiasm for male attention, she might actually have a chance at enduring happiness. So, since she's made a conscious decision to change her behavior, Stacey interacts with Jonathan in a way that makes him feel exceptional, desirable, and highly esteemed by her. Even though she used to encourage male attention in the past, she actively discourages it, especially when she's with Jonathan.

For example, at social gatherings, when Jonathan leaves momentarily to get drinks, she politely rejects other men when they try to engage her in conversation. If she and Jonathan are together and an old flame sees her and attempts to get her attention, she does not allow the ex to linger past a courteous introduction and farewell. When she's with Jonathan and men pay her passing compliments, if they're appropriate she simply says, "thank you." If they're not appropriate or respectful of Jonathan, she ignores them entirely, grasps Jonathan's arm tighter, and momentarily leans her head against his shoulder. Even if other highly attractive men stare at her or try to make eye contact with her, she ignores them as if they simply do not exist in her world. She also ignores the "friend-zoned" men in her life when they try to buy her gifts, perform favors, or ask her out. In short, because she respects Jonathan and values their blossoming relationship, she does not encourage the attention of other men nor does she incite their interest in her.

High-quality men like Jonathan, when they're auditioning women for a life of love and commitment, will quietly observe you to assess your capacity for loyalty. When a woman makes it clear that she has eyes for us and us alone, especially when other more successful, physically fit, charming, or higher-status men are around, it makes us want her even more.

If a guy is testing your loyalty, constantly entertaining other men won't keep him interested unless he enjoys dating women who "play" hard-to-get. In general, men don't like women who play hard-to-get per se. When we're searching for a long-term mate, what we really desire is the unconditional love and loyalty of a woman who IS hard-to-get (or better yet, impossible-to-get) for *other* men. Remember that.

14

Temper your desire for a man so that you don't become blind to the defects in his character. A woman's longing, if left unchecked by reason, leads to desperation. And female desperation, being highly susceptible to a man's charms, leads to blind infatuation.

You're on your sixth date with a very attractive, successful, and charismatic man who takes charge and seems to know what he wants. You love this about him and if you're being honest, you've never felt so drawn to a guy like this since, well...ever! Based on his actions, you know he's really into you as well and you can't help but fantasize about a possible future with this particular Prince Charming. He treats you with kindness and has been nothing but an absolute gentleman to you. He's even kind with waiters, parking attendants, and the other strangers you inevitably meet on your various dates.

However, on this particular date, you notice something about him that you didn't pick up at first, something that makes you feel extremely uneasy about him. The reason you didn't pick it up at first was because this is the first date you've been on with him in which he's had to interact with people he already knows. He's finally invited you out with his friends, and as you watch him interact with them you begin to realize that your Prince Charming, as charming and masculine as he is, doesn't seem to reserve his kindness for those closest to him.

You notice he's a bit harsh with his friends and hardly lets anyone else get a word in during "group" conversation. You notice that he's quick to shut down and dismiss his friends' opinions, and that he even gets miffed whenever someone disagrees with him. In a moment of shock, your eyes widen when you hear him refer to another friend (one not present) by a name that most people, yourself included, consider highly derogatory. You're sitting there wondering, *"Why do his friends put up with him?"* and you're beginning to get that gut feeling that you will surely become a second-class citizen in your own relationship if you two ever to become exclusive.

At this point, you've already decided that you won't be going on a seventh date, that is...until Mr. Prince Charming touches the small of your back, leans into you, and whispers something in your ears that makes your pulse quicken and your heart race all at once. You blush incessantly and, forgetting what had previously preoccupied your mind, you start gazing lovingly into his eyes as if he'd just bought you the moon.

What did he tell you? It doesn't matter really. Your interest in him was stoked by *what he said* to you, and it completely trumped *what his behavior* was revealing at the moment. You chose to ignore the warning signs and followed how he made you *feel* instead. Whatever he said to you stirred your feminine desire and convinced you to continue seeing him. It was powerful and personal enough to override the evidence you had just gathered regarding your Prince Charming's less than charming behavior towards those close to him.

The thing is, when we have strong emotions for someone or something we use logic merely as a support system to make ourselves feel better about our wants. Thus, when we're highly attracted to someone, we use logic to supply us with reasons *why* we like, want, and should be with that person. Desire or, the euphoric emotions someone makes us feel, is a poor tool for judging whether or not they can make us happy in a long-term sense.

For example, a young lady who has an insatiable passion for the latest in designer heels doesn't need a plethora of reasons why she wants the newest pair. She just wants them. And after she's purchased them, if asked why she "needed" them, she can give you a host of reasons why it was an excellent purchase, even if the shoes are grossly expensive, impractical for everyday usage, and can only go with one of her dresses.

Similar to this young lady and her shoe obsessions, you might allow the passion and excitement you feel for a man to guide your decision to continue dating him. Total reliance on the chemistry you feel with him ultimately leads you into a turbulent relationship where, once the passion cools, you realize your Prince Charming was all show and no substance. He was just another "shiny object" who distracted you with his good looks, charm, and a commanding presence. So, what's the moral here? Simple. Never allow the raw desire you feel for a particular guy to completely dominate your sense of reason, as it will continually thwart your efforts to identify a man worth dating vs. a complete waste a time.

15

Be responsive and keep an open mind if a desirable and familiar gentleman invites you on a date via text message. Be sure, however, that as the relationship matures, so does his method of making plans with you. Be wary of men who insist on inviting you out on dates predominantly through texting.

Depending on your age and the nature in which you regularly keep in contact with the men you date, your mileage may vary with this particular guideline. That being said, you should be wary of men who predominantly use text messages to make dating plans throughout the course of your relationship with him. The reason being is because texting is an exceptionally useful tool for men who are more likely to be romantically lazy, juggling several women at once, or who are simply using you to pass the time. Granted, I'm not saying that ALL men who primarily text you to make plans are players and time wasters, but it is highly likely that a good majority of them will be.

The effective approach is to be responsive and indulgent with men who text you for dates in the beginning while ensuring that they progress to calling you more often to make plans as the relationship develops. If you have been going out with a guy for at least several weeks and he still insists on ONLY texting you to make plans, you need to gracefully enlighten him that you'd prefer to *hear* from him, literally, the next time he wants to meet up with you. Remember, just because a man's behavior is subpar at first doesn't necessarily mean that he's a lost cause. The right man, your Mr. Right so to speak, will be the man who isn't afraid of your standards. Instead, he will find your dating standards profoundly refreshing, as it will challenge him to enhance his efforts if he truly wants to conquer your heart.

Now, I totally understand that for many women, accepting a first date via text seems like they're cheapening themselves. You may feel like this especially if you have a very traditional and high-class view of courtship between a man and a woman. Believe me, I completely understand if you would never go out with a guy who asks you out via text, especially for a first date. But before you write off every man who acts this way, you should at least consider the reality of today's tech-influenced dating landscape.

The reason you want to stay open-minded, at least in the beginning, is because of how times have changed in the last several years regarding how we humans communicate using technology. A decade or so ago, having a guy text you out for a first date was a sure sign that he couldn't be *that* serious about dating a woman of your calibre. Today, however, because texting has become the preferred method of communicating among a good majority of the smartphone carrying population, having a guy ask you out on a first date via text isn't necessarily a sign that he's bad news.

So, if you're a twenty or thirty-something year old woman, having an attractive acquaintance or a dashing gentleman that you've previously met text you for a first date shouldn't set off any "red flags" regarding his seriousness, romantic interests, or intentions. On the other hand, if you're over the age of forty-five or so, it does seem a bit tasteless if a gentleman around your age or older texts you for a first date. Again, your mileage with this guideline might vary based on your personal taste and communication preferences. But no matter your age, you would still be wise to take these insights and guidelines into consideration.

16

Be an excellent receiver. While a woman should be appreciative of a man's kindness towards her, she should never feel obligated to reciprocate such kindness with her most private generosities or pleasures.

Is it possible for a woman to be *too* nice? Yes. Yes, it is. And in no other dating situation is this more prevalent than when a woman feels obligated to do or give something special to a man just because he has been "nice" to her. While I always encourage women to be as kind and as generous as possible with the men they date, **I also caution them *not* to lower their standards or allow men to cross their boundaries while doing so**.

It is *very* easy to make allowances for someone we're deeply attracted to, especially if they are "nice" to us. If they do or give something special to us, we might feel compelled to return the favor in an effort to show our appreciation. While there's nothing inherently wrong with this behavior, things can get out of hand rather quickly if your boundaries aren't crystal clear regarding the limits to your generosity.

There should be certain things that you simply will not do for a man you have only been dating several weeks. There should be certain things that you simply will not do for a man who isn't your boyfriend. There should also be certain things that you will not do for a man who isn't your husband. And if you're particularly aware of your standards, there should even be things you simply won't do for any man…no matter what kind of relationship you have with him. When you're clear about such things beforehand, it's a lot easier to stick to your guns and say "No" or "No thanks", especially in situations where you feel that a man's kindness may come with a price you are unwilling to pay.

The reality is, in the early stages of dating you have no idea what your Mr. McDreamy is really after. You haven't had sufficient time with him to fully assess his character, his compatibility with you, and his capacity for a commitment. Therefore, you should not feel pressured or compelled to repay his kindness towards you with extravagant favors of any kind, whether they are material or even sexual in nature.

Just because a man shows you kindness in the beginning doesn't mean he's kind-hearted. I mean, even if he IS kind-hearted, it still doesn't mean he's already determined that you're the only woman deserving of his kindness. He could be kind to you today and gone tomorrow. And I'm sure we can agree that his going would be a lot less painful if you keep yourself from giving him too much of your charity way too soon.

Don't be nice to a guy just for the sake of being nice or even to keep him interested in you. Be nice to him because you want to and because you feel empowered when doing so. If your generosity towards a man disempowers you in that you're left feeling humiliated or dishonored, you're probably being overly generous with a man who either doesn't deserve it yet or doesn't deserve it at all.

Give a man time to prove to you that he deserves access to your most private generosities. Remember, if you don't value or highly treasure what it is you have to offer a man, neither will he.

17

Always be straightforward and sincere when a man asks you about your relationship desires and aspirations. Though your honesty may turn off some men, it is better to lose the interest of an incompatible suitor sooner than later.

Never feign disinterest for a committed relationship if that is what you truly want. Hiding the fact that you want to be in a committed relationship is a terrible strategy for keeping a man interested in you. Many women neglect to tell men what they want in a relationship usually out of fear. The fear of scaring a potentially great guy away causes them to keep quiet about their truest relationship desires, which ultimately leads them into dead-end relationships or dead-on-arrival romances with time-wasting men.

When a new guy asks you about your relationship desires and aspirations…tell him. Don't pretend as if you have none in an attempt to make him feel unpressured. Telling him what you want in a relationship has nothing to do with him. It's about *your* desires and *your* standards. So, don't worry about "pressuring him". You should feel free to express exactly what kind of relationship you'd like to experience with your ideal man…whether that ideal man is him or not.

If you reveal your relationship desires with class and sincerity, most men aren't going to run for the nearest exit or go radio silent on you after you've expressed yourself. The key to communicating your wants with confidence is to ensure that you speak with that warm, feminine, heartfelt sincerity that men love and adore. Don't hem and haw or hesitate to share your desires. Just be true to your feelings and express yourself with the utmost womanly poise.

For example, it is totally reasonable for a woman to respond to a man's curiosities with something like, *"I'm interested in a relationship that progresses toward a commitment when the time is right."* This is a simple, laid-back response that is especially useful for women who are deathly afraid of telling men what they want. Of course, if you also want to express your desire for marriage in the future without coming off as being overly eager about it, you could try this simple variation: *"I'm interested in a relationship that progresses toward a commitment when the time is right. And at some point in the future, possibly marriage."*

Of course, if you're a bit more confident (and particularly sassy) when communicating with men, you might want to say or text something like: *"I want a relationship with a man who will eventually commit to me because he wants me all to himself."* (Remember to toss in a flirty wink at the end of that sentence if you're texting it.) Most red-blooded men will LOVE this response simply because it communicates your wants clearly while playfully insinuating that when a man does commit to you it will be because he can't get enough of you. Men love it when a woman expresses herself in ways that cultivates both their respect AND their desire for her at the same time.

Now, keep in mind that when a new guy openly asks you about what you want in a relationship it means he is genuinely trying to figure out if your relationship goals are in line with his own. This is a man who is probably less likely to waste your time because he wants to find out as quickly as possible which "love interest" category he should place you in. If he's the kind of guy who is sincerely looking for love, giving him a vague or divertive answer about what you want in a relationship might cause him to "friend-zone" and lose interest in you almost immediately. On the other hand, if he's the kind of guy who is open to either a commitment or even "something in between", giving him a vague or divertive answer will make him see you as more of a potential "friend-with-benefits" than a future girlfriend. This is the reality of how a man's mind will work if a woman appears unclear or uncertain of what she wants.

You see, when a man takes a romantic interest in a woman he begins running two very different

subconscious "mating objectives" at the same time. One of these mating objectives is focused on short-term sexual conquest while the other is focused on long-term mate selection. The information a woman provides a man during the time he spends with her will unconsciously dictate to him the best category to place her in. This is true for ALL men. This is why it is extremely important to communicate your high-standards from the beginning of a new romance and even as it progresses.

Men's brains are naturally wired to ascertain and appraise a woman's value as a romantic partner. From the moment a man meets you, he begins evaluating your status in comparison to his own as well as your overall significance as a potential sexual partner and romantic companion. This is one of the reasons why it is vitally important to tell a man exactly what you are looking for in a relationship. Confidently telling him that you want a relationship that progresses towards commitment, tells him that you are very aware of your high-value as a romantic partner. Telling him this also shows him that the bar for his performance has already been set, which means it's now up to him to decide if he's up to the challenge or not.

Don't hesitate to tell a man exactly what kind of relationship you want, especially if he asks. If you are vague or dismissive about your relationship desires you might sabotage your chances at finding a man who wants the kind of relationship you want as well. In the least, your fearless candor will gain the respect of the men you come across, including those who may have only wanted something short-term with you. Hence, no matter the outcome, it is always more advantageous for a woman to be upfront about what she wants in a relationship.

61

18

Beware of the "sunk cost" fallacy that convinces many women to remain in unfulfilling relationships. Don't be afraid to call it quits on a dead investment early on. If a man has consistently proved himself to be unworthy of her love, a woman must be willing to walk away.

When a guy suddenly tells you that he wants to be "just friends…with benefits" or he tries to seduce you into some other kind of dead-end relationship, can you walk away from him…for good? I'm not talking about some random guy whom you are barely interested in. I'm talking about your alleged dream guy who is attractive, successful, exudes masculine sexual confidence, and says all the right things to intoxicate you with desire. Can you walk away from your "alleged" dream guy, one whom you've already fallen for or even have a relationship with, if he attempts to make you a friend-with-benefits? Can you seriously walk away from your supposed Mr. Right if you come to realize that he's incapable of reciprocating your love?

The "sunk cost" fallacy occurs when we allow our past investment of time, emotions, resources, etc., to interfere with our decision-making in the present, usually in ways that prove detrimental to our future. When we make present-day decisions based on the hopeful future value of something we've invested our time, energy, money, etc., we tend to misjudge. Our decisions are tainted by our past emotional investment, and thus we overestimate the benefits and value something might bring us in the future. There is no better example of the "sunk cost" fallacy at work than in romantic relationships.

If you have made a significant amount of emotional investment in a guy, it can be extremely difficult to disregard that investment when you realize that the guy you're dating turned out to be nothing more than a liability. But while this might tempt you to hold course so that you can "see where this thing goes", don't give in to that temptation. It will only allow him to waste your time even further.

If a man has consistently proven himself to be unworthy of your love, the love you have already put into the relationship is now nothing more than a sunk cost that must be ignored. Trying to "honor" the sunk costs (time spent, tears cried, love shared, gifts bought, trips taken, etc.) by staying in a bad relationship in hopes that a man will change is a terrible decision. And unfortunately for women, it's a decision that many men continue to exploit at their leisure.

Many women also seem to struggle with the idea of walking away from a man they consider high-value or "perfect" in some way, shape, or form. They will put up with his emotional unavailability, his half-hearted attempts to keep in touch, and even his cheating if they're desperate enough. When a woman fails to properly recognize and preserve her own value, she may end up attaching her value to the man she's with. Her self-worth then becomes centered on the supposed quality of the man she's dating. And when this hold becomes strong enough, she may find herself unwilling to leave a dead-end relationship so long as it gives her access to and attention from the man she so highly esteems.

The major flaw in her thinking in this regard is that her lack of self-respect causes her to attach her sense of worth to the quality or "rightness" of the man in her life. Because she's so focused on the "rightness" of the man she's dating, she pays little attention for the "rightness" of the relationship and whether or not her dream guy is actually making her happy.

The key to being able to walk away from a "shiny object" is to ensure that your dream guy, or Mr. Right, is also Mr. Commitment-Compatible. In one of the points from my book, *Never Chase Men Again*, I discuss the importance of appraising the men you date based on both their inner qualities and the compatibility of your dating and relationship goals. If your alleged Mr. Right has all the right qualities, all the right assets, and all the right moves but doesn't want the kind of commitment you want, guess what? He's not really Mr. Right. Waiting around for him to change his mind in hopes that you will eventually lull him into a serious commitment is an extraordinarily bad idea.

You must learn to place equal importance on a man's relationship goals as opposed to just the man himself. Keeping this standard firmly in mind will keep you from falling head-over-heels in love with a man who might be seemingly perfect, but unable to reciprocate your love and devotion. Remember, it's extremely difficult to walk away from something that lends you self-worth. Because like all "lenders", it will eventually own you entirely and perhaps even destroy you in the process. So be careful not to attach your self-esteem to being with a particular type of man.

As human beings, we tend to have strong feelings for things we're deeply emotionally invested in, even if they're slowly killing us or making us miserable. Our brains have a way of tricking us into believing that moving on from a dead investment is a bad idea because it confirms that we made a grave error and thus have wasted our most precious resource: our time. However, in reality, dealing shrewdly with sunk costs is a common aspect of everyone's life, and those who learn how to detach their emotions from their past investments will be able to move on to better things.

It's easy to place too much hope in the future if you have already invested so much of yourself in a relationship. This is true whether you've been passionately dating a guy for two weeks, two months, or even two years. Even so, try to resist the temptation to "honor" your sunk costs, and never be afraid to let go and move on when a man is either incapable or unwilling to reciprocate your love, no matter how otherwise "perfect" he may seem.

Chapter Three:

The Beliefs and Standards of High-Value Women

19

Be firm but gracious when communicating your limits with men. The key to expressing your boundaries or rebuffing a man's premature sexual advances in an attractive way is to allude to your desire for him while setting your standard.

Never be afraid to enforce your personal boundaries or express your limitations with a man. Being able to do so with poise and decorum will subconsciously communicate to him that you are a high-value woman, one who has standards and reasonable expectations. Women who can confidently tell a man what they want and don't want are rare and therefore VERY sought after.

Unfortunately, many women are terrified to set boundaries with a man they're highly attracted to because they fear that he'll lose interest, withdraw, or become completely turned off. These women believe that telling a man "No" or shutting down his premature sexual advances might drive away a potential boyfriend. If you struggle to set boundaries with men due to a deep fear of potential loss, you can stop worrying about it. Your fear of loss is groundless, and here's why: The men who won't be turned off by your limits are the ones who will cherish you the most.

Of course, if you are worried about coming across as being "too demanding" or "not interested enough", try to use the "firm but enticing" technique. When you must express your limitations or outright reject a man's advances, simply state how you feel but use a hint of seduction to keep him intrigued. Here's a simple yet powerful step-by-step communication method for accomplishing this:

1. Compliment him by telling him how he makes you feel. The best way to do this is to say something genuine about him that singles him out as being "better" than other men in some way.

2. Communicate your boundaries and tell him "No" in a clear but courteous way.

3. Express to him why the boundary is important to you.

For example, if a man is trying to be too sexually forward with you, it's one thing to tell him, *"No, I'm not ready,"* and another thing to tell him, *"Listen, Mike, I like you. A lot. I mean...you make me feel things I've never felt for any man before. But I'm not ready for this yet. I want to give myself to the man who wants me for a lifetime. I hope you understand."*

Did you see the difference there?

The first boundary setting is perfectly fine, but it won't make his mind burn with anticipation and curiosity like the second one. And if "Mike" considers himself to be a potential "lifetime lover" candidate, he'll do whatever he can to prove to you that he's the man for job, no matter how long it takes.

By using the firm but enticing technique you'll communicate your limits and make **the right man** desperate to see you again all at the same time. Men don't mind being rejected once it's done with grace and respect for their ego. A man is less likely to see your rejection as a sign of your "lack of interest" if you can communicate your boundaries with a sincere expression of desire.

Certain situations won't call for a firm and enticing response, however. Sometimes you might just need to be firm. In cases where a man is unknowingly (or knowingly) disrespecting you, acting too sexually aggressive, or taking you for granted, you need to be firm. Let him know where he stands with you and make it clear that YOU don't like or appreciate the way you're being treated. Just ensure that you own your feelings and don't cast blame. For example, saying *"**You** never take me out anymore, **you** don't care about me do **you**?"* is casting blame and won't win you any awards with men. Instead, say, *"**I feel** as if **I'm** not a priority to you anymore. **I** really enjoy it when you take me dancing or to dinner. **I'd** really like it if we did something fun this weekend!"*

See the difference?

The first response will make him feel inadequate and might even cause him to pull away from you, as he will begin to think that he's incapable of making you happy. The second response is that of an emotionally mature woman who takes responsibility for her own her feelings rather than casting blame on a man. She also communicates her high-value by being specific about what she needs from her guy in order to be happy in the relationship.

Don't be misled into thinking that men will find you too difficult if you enforce your boundaries or express your relationship needs. We WANT to make you happy, and the more clear and courteous you are with us about what makes you happy, **the happier we are about making you happy**.

Communicating your limits and relationship needs in a way that men perceive as being "high-value" is crucial to keeping a man interested for the long-term. So, don't worry about turning men off with your needs and expectations (assuming they're reasonable). You're more likely to lose a guy's interest if you neglect to express your personal boundaries. And remember, when you state what it is you will and won't accept a man should be thoroughly convinced of your stance but not offended by your delivery. Sure, he may feel hurt or even upset at the interaction if it isn't in his favor, but his dissatisfaction should come from him not getting his way as opposed to him feeling disrespected or undesired.

20

Never make yourself a fool for flaky male behavior. If you allow a man to flake on you once, he will most assuredly do it again...and again...and again.

In the event you're not familiar with the term, a "flake" is basically someone who doesn't follow through. They are major procrastinators, highly unreliable, and nearly incapable of keeping their word. The major factor in determining whether or not a flake will actually follow through is based on his or her *mood* at the time or the *urgency* of the need to act. In short, flakes make terrible friends and disastrous partners (both in love and in business) to those unfortunate enough to rely on them.

But what are the telling behaviors of the flaky male specimen in a dating situation? Below I've listed a few of the most common examples of flaky behavior a man might unknowingly display when interacting with a woman:

- He becomes wishy-washy with his attention and might even break off contact with you as soon as you begin showing a serious interest in him.

- He disappears from time to time or does not respond in a **reasonable amount of time** when communicating with you, and does not give a valid explanation for doing so.

- He cancels dates on short notice without suggesting a future date to make up for it.

- He arrives unreasonably late and gives off an attitude of indifference towards his tardiness.

- He defends his flakiness with the belief that he "doesn't owe you anything" and that he can "do as he pleases", in spite of the fact you've already made significant investments of love and loyalty towards him.

- He does not follow through on his word and usually gives a dishonest excuse for doing so. That is, if he actually cares enough to provide an excuse at all.

Simply put, a man who flakes on you does not hold you in high regard. If he doesn't hold you in high regard, he does not deserve your attention. It doesn't really matter "why" he flaked, as men flake on women for a myriad of reasons that could span a book of its own (most of those reasons have nothing to do with you by the way). All you need to concern yourself with is how *you* respond to Flaky Frank moving forward. Once you realize that a guy isn't respectful of your time and attention, you must cease to entertain him and turn your attention to more persistent admirers.

And for heaven's sake, do not give a flake your sympathy. For example, if a guy cancels a date at the last minute and, even though he offers you a seemingly valid excuse does not reschedule the date, do not suggest a rescheduling yourself. If he doesn't reschedule the date, resist the temptation to make things easy for him. Taking the initiative to reschedule the date yourself will come off as a sign of desperation, and you'll soon find yourself playing the ugly game of Chase-a-Man. Also, don't drum up an excuse for him in your mind so that you'll feel less guilty about suggesting another date and time. Don't make excuses for him and don't text or call him to "see if he wants to try again." Doing so will immediately inform a man that he holds a higher place of importance in your mind than you do in his. And if you weren't already aware of it, this is not the position a woman wants to be in, especially in the early stages of dating.

So, if you value your sanity, here's my advice: Do not tolerate the company of men who consistently flake out on you. It doesn't matter how dreamy you think he is or how reasonable his excuses seem. If a guy cancels dates, changes plans, never shows up, or consistently neglects to call you **when he said he would**, you are dealing with a man-flake and thus, you must treat him accordingly.

21

The high-value woman does not accept unreasonable tardiness without a reasonable excuse.

Let's say a handsome gentleman (we'll call him Mr. Handsome Face) you met through a friend of a friend has finally asked you out on a date. Let's also say that he tells you he's going to pick you up on Friday night at eight o'clock sharp. Excitedly, you prepare for the date well in advance with some long over-due personal beautification and you even borrow a gorgeous outfit from one of your close friends (you know, the one who has ALL the clothes you like).

Friday evening arrives and you eagerly wait for Mr. Handsome Face to show up. Seven thirty rolls by and you're almost done getting ready. Seven fifty rolls by, and you're done-up proper and waiting patiently on your couch trying to read a novel to distract yourself. Eight o'clock rolls by and you're expecting him to knock on your door at any moment. Eight fifteen rolls by and naturally, you're getting a little over-anxious. Eight thirty rolls by and now you're getting a little concerned. Nine o'clock creeps along and suddenly you hear a knock at your door. Pop quiz time! Do you:

A. Ignore his tardiness and go on the date anyway.

B. Graciously ask for an explanation for his tardiness and then **politely** refuse the date if he doesn't have one.

C. Throw a drink in his face right before you slam the door on him.

As a self-possessed woman of class, I'm going to assume you went with B, as B is truly the only option if you want to communicate to a man that your attention is valuable and that your good-graces are not cheap commodities. Accepting a man's extreme tardiness without a reasonable excuse will go beyond him thinking that you're "easy-going", he'll simply think you're "easy." Not having standards or setting boundaries when it comes to your attention forces a man to make a value judgment about you that tells him: She's not worth my best wooing efforts.

Let's be real here. Being unreasonably late to meet someone or do something is basically bad manners no matter the situation, and thus it isn't the kind of behavior anyone should encourage. If you consistently entertain such behavior you will find that people will not respect your time, which ultimately means that they do not respect you. The same applies when it comes to a fresh romance. If you begin making allowances for a guy early on without some sort of polite penalty or gracious reprimand, **he will not value the attention you give him** and thus, he will not respect you. And if you don't know by now, a man will not commit his all to a woman if he does not respect her.

Now, there are two things you should be mindful of when determining if you are still going to go out with Mr. Handsome Face despite his lateness. The first thing is whether his excuse is actually reasonable. The second thing concerns the magnitude of his tardiness.

Unfortunately, I cannot tell you what a "reasonable excuse" is or not; it depends entirely on the circumstance. For example, if his excuse is that he had to work extra late at the last minute to finish something for his boss, you would be within your right to wonder why he did not at least call you to say that he would be a little late. But if he says he had to work late AND that his phone battery died meaning he had no way of reaching you, *this* excuse is quite reasonable. You must judge his earnestness for yourself in such cases because sometimes all kind of crazy things can happen to get in the way of love. As you listen to his excuse, be sure that his attitude is sincerely regretful about his tardiness rather than flippant.

Determining how late is "too late" is another thing you should consider. For instance, five minutes too late is fine. Even ten minutes too late is still in the domain of "excusable" in most cases. Beyond fifteen minutes too late, however, you should be expecting some sort of excuse or apology. And at thirty minutes too late you're not being "unreasonable" if you decide to cancel the date IF he doesn't have a reasonable excuse.

Of course, I do understand that it might be extremely difficult to turn away seemingly eligible bachelors if you haven't had a date (or a quality boyfriend) in a long, long time. If you're not that confident about when the next ship (guy) is coming in, you might want to take the "One Date Test Run" approach. If Mr. Handsome Face arrives later than is reasonable and has an even *less* reasonable excuse, consider accepting the date knowing in the back of your mind that he'll have to pull out all the stops to win back your good-graces. Now, when I say, "win back your good-graces" I'm not saying you should be mean, disrespectful, indifferent, or even unenthusiastic while you're out with him. What I *do* mean is that you're free to enjoy the evening knowing that he has ONE shot to impress you or else you're never going to see him again. Is this a cold-hearted approach? No. Is it a cutthroat approach? Absolutely.

If a guy shows up late with a flimsy excuse (assuming he has one) and you still go out with him, you need to be extra judicious. You're not leading him on by accepting the date knowing that there's a low chance he'll get another, you're just granting him the opportunity to re-earn your respect while giving yourself the opportunity to discover love. If love happens and sparks fly, so be it. If it turns out his shameless tardiness was just the tip of the iceberg regarding his lack of character, so be it. Like I always say, don't be afraid to take risks when it comes to romance, but always be willing to walk away from a dead-end investment as quickly and as graciously as you can.

Again, as with all the points in this book, use your discretion and trust your woman's intuition when it comes to men and dating. If you think his excuse is mediocre and he showed up thirty minutes late, then by all means go out with him if you still get an overall "good vibe" from him. If you think his excuse is flimsy, but he showed up forty minutes late with a well-thought out apology gift, if you *really* like him, then by all means go out with him. Just keep in mind that setting the standard that you will not make allowances for unreasonable tardiness early on is a helpful way to set apart the serious suitors from those who might ultimately waste your time.

22

Do not tolerate men who show indifference towards your tender display of emotions. Use your emotional vulnerabilities to test a man's compassion, esteem, and earnestness of affection for you. Only the man with a kindred soul will be drawn to you even more when you share your soul with him.

One of the most effective things you can do to determine if a man is genuinely interested in you is to share your vulnerable side with him, then observe how he responds to you (assuming he responds at all). Of course, you don't have to confess your deepest darkest secrets to him, but instead, share private little intimacies with him that you wouldn't share with the average person. Such private merriments and concerns may include but aren't limited to:

- Cherished childhood memories.

- Painful memories from your past, such as a friend's betrayal.

- Present-day struggles, such as your fear of switching careers or the issues you're having with a co-worker.

- Quirky interests that you're passionate (or

obsessed) about.

- Things that make you deeply emotional in any way, such as mistreated pets, domestic violence, your church's ministry, or your sister's rehab journey.

If you open up about such things and Mr. Tall-Dark-and-Handsome doesn't appear even remotely interested, moved, or engaged with what you're saying, he's probably not as into you as you would have hoped. When a man has a *sincere* romantic interest in a woman, he won't be able to hide his sympathies and enthusiasms whenever she shares the beautiful varieties of her emotions with him.

Truth is, getting emotional with the man you're dating will either frighten him away (Mr. Wrong) or draw him closer to you (Mr. Right), so you cannot lose with this strategy. Becoming vulnerable with a guy allows him to catch glimpses of your soul. And if he's Mr. Right he'll become even more curious and infatuated with you over time. He will see you as a "kindred soul" so to speak, and will feel even more emotionally drawn to you in the process.

Now, my only caveat with this approach is to be sure that you are only showing 'glimpses' into your soul. Things can easily backfire if you spew out the contents of your heart all in one go. Doing so can potentially frighten guys away if you're not discerning with your approach. You want to reveal just enough of your heart to see if he can engage with you on an emotional level, but not so much that he feels overwhelmed all at once.

In my book, *The 7 Irresistible Qualities Men Want In A Woman*, I stress the point that what a man really wants is an *emotional experience* with a great woman, and he can only enjoy this level of intimacy when a woman is willing to be vulnerable with him. You have to be willing to give him glimpses of your heart (the good, bad, and bizarre) *without shame or regret*. If a man takes an interest in the precious, peculiar, and problematic things that both lighten and burden your heart, he's worth your time. Even more so, if he connects with your vulnerability by showing you his own, he might even be a keeper.

23

You do not tolerate entertaining a man solely out of boredom, loneliness, or a need to validate your desirability. If you are convinced that there is no future with him, do not waste your time or his.

As stated in the introduction, this book was written mainly to assist women who aren't just dating to find their next boyfriend (and thus their next ex), but who actually want to find their Mr. Right and eventually get married. So, with the assumption that finding a commitment-minded, high-quality man to someday marry is your end goal, you're going to have a much easier time avoiding dead-end relationships and missed opportunities by dating with more integrity and purposefulness than the average woman. What this means is resisting the temptation to entice or entertain men when you KNOW you don't see or want a future with them.

Just because there are tons of men out there and you find yourself spoiled for choice does not mean that the men you date are disposable. If you find yourself losing interest in a potential suitor, dismiss him graciously. Treat every man you encounter with respect and kindness on your dating journey. The moment you treat a man in a way that shows little regard for his self-worth, you prove yourself to be just as basic as any other woman.

Of course, just like every other human being on this planet, from time to time you may find yourself bored, lonely, and mired in self-doubt. If you haven't been in a steady, fulfilling relationship in quite some time, you may even be more prone to such feelings. But even though such emotions have the propensity to lead us into short-term, unfulfilling pseudo-relationships to pass the time, it doesn't mean we should allow them to do this.

I was chatting with a female friend of mine awhile back who had recently begun dating another friend of mine. I have known these two individuals for years, and I was both surprised and excited that they had gotten together and were now in a committed relationship.

Since I had known this young lady for so long, I was very familiar with some of her dating past. So out of curiosity, I asked her what made her present relationship with my friend so different and more purposeful than her past pseudo-relationships. She responded by admitting that my friend (the guy she was seeing) had a more mature energy about him that made it clear he was actively looking for someone with whom he could settle down. She also said that SHE was also in a more mature place in her life where **she knew what she wanted and**

would not allow any man, my friend included, to give her the run around and waste her time.

She decided that if he didn't want to be with her she would make room in her life for a man who did. She also said that looking back, if she was really honest with herself, her taste in men and her dating behavior made her attract guys who only wanted something short-term. She admitted that she foolishly entertained men and relationships she *knew* weren't going anywhere, but she kept seeing them anyway because she was having fun.

Wow.

Needless to say, I was impressed by her response as it showed her maturity and ripened sense of self-respect. But what really impressed me was her admission that in the past she didn't realize she was attracting like-minded, and thus time-wasting men by default. Although she might have wanted men to take her seriously, her subconscious desire to "have fun" had a stronger influence on the kinds of men she attracted as well as her tolerance of them.

I say all of this to point out that you cannot have a "vague" desire or wish to be with a mature, relationship-minded man who sees you as a prize-worth-pursuing. You have to have a clear mental vision of the kind of relationship you want AND you must ensure that your present-day actions aren't creating a strong dissonance in your mind. For example, if you consistently tell yourself (and everyone else) that all you really want is a committed relationship with a mature, loving, kind-hearted, masculine guy, your behavior towards men (and yourself) must coincide with what you want. If you entertain men out of boredom, loneliness, or to validate your desirability, you're training yourself to *accept* less than what you really want.

It's one thing to accidently waste time on a guy because he sold you a dream, but it's another thing to consciously waste time on him because you were bored, lonely, or lacking self-confidence. So, while there's nothing wrong with having as much fun as possible on your dating journey to find Mr. Right, just be mindful of what you consistently accept and tolerate. If you realize that the men you have been allowing into your life no longer measure up with what you presently believe about yourself...cease to entertain them.

If you want men to treat you with respect, love, kindness, and dignity, be the better woman and treat the guys you come across the exact same way. Resist the temptation to lie to yourself if you choose to entertain men and relationships that have zero to little potential. Such "relationships" will get you nowhere fast and you will only end up getting so comfortable that you won't have the emotional hunger needed to find Mr. Right. Entertaining pseudo-relationships with men you either don't want or don't see a future with will keep you unfulfilled and comfortable at best. In fact, you'll end up being so comfortable that your attempts to search for something better will be half-hearted at best. This is one of the biggest reasons why many women who "want" to find Mr. Right remain stuck dating Mr. Right-Now.

Listen, drastic changes demand drastic decisions. So, don't be afraid to get out of your comfort zone. You cannot expect to change the status of your love life overnight if what you want and what you actually allow and tolerate simply don't coincide. While you *should* aim to have as much fun as humanly possible while trying to find Mr. Right, remember to hold yourself to a higher standard and date purposefully.

24

Do not blame yourself or submit to your anger when a man treats you with disinterest or disrespect. Instead, see subpar male behavior as an opportunity to illustrate your high self-worth, to cultivate attraction with a man, and to test his resolve to be with you.

The way a woman defines a situation defines her reality. If a man's negative behavior makes you loosen your standards or lose your composure, it means you're prone to attaching "negative-meanings" to situations in which men don't act the way you want them to. This makes it easy for you to fall into the 'victim' role, which ultimately leaves you powerless when it comes to getting what you want from men. However, if a man's negative behavior compels you to reassess your own behavior or recalibrate your interactions with him, it means that you regularly attach positive-meanings to the unwelcomed dating situations you might experience.

One of the secrets to winning with men when things don't go your way is to keep your composure, enforce your boundaries, and *reframe* the situation to show that you are the better person. Men are status driven creatures, and thus, when a woman successfully shows herself to be "the better woman", a man cannot help but to feel both respect and adoration for her. Assuming his interest is sincere, a high-quality man is less likely to walk away from a woman who confidently held her ground with him.

The key to responding to a man's disinterest or disrespect, at the highest level, is to see every instance of negative male behavior as an opportunity to demonstrate your substance. For example, instead of blaming yourself and loosening your standards the minute a highly eligible bachelor attempts to make you a friend-with-benefits, shake his reality by rejecting his invitation outright and telling him you're not interested in being a part of his harem, or anyone else's. Follow this up by admitting that you thought he was different, and that you're still grateful he revealed his true taste in women early on instead of leading you on indefinitely. And lastly, thank him for the good time he showed you.

I know. I know. The above response isn't something most women can do with a straight, non-murderous face. But this is exactly the kind of response that communicates a woman's high-value and unshakeable resolve to date by a higher standard.

The guy in the situation above will be baffled. In fact, if he's particularly experienced with women, he might have expected you to:

1. Compromise your standards to keep him in your life, or…

2. Lose your cool entirely and tell him how you hope he takes a flying leap off the nearest skyscraper.

Most guys will expect one of the above responses. The highest value response is so rare from a woman, that it can sometimes shock a man into reality and force him to question his own behavior. Men of today aren't used to getting a graceful, challenging response after rejecting a woman. This is why *reframing* the situation to illustrate his inability to make you happy is so powerful. When a man's pulling away cannot pull you apart, it makes him look at you in a different light.

Now I will admit, doing this successfully, especially in the heat of the moment, requires practice. In fact, the best practice is to do this in every area of your life, where you reframe negative, unwanted situations as opportunities to be "the better woman" and illustrate your high-value. If you have been prone to attaching negative-meanings to undesirable situations with men in the past, your new behavior will take a while to stick. But as with anything else in life, in time, practice will make perfect.

So just to clarify, here are the two things you should never do when you find yourself on the receiving end of a man's disinterest or disrespect:

1. Do not blame yourself or view the relationship failure as you being "not enough" for a man. Blaming yourself gives an enormous amount of power to your insecurities and it will cause you to act irrationally to soothe the pain. Women who blame themselves and who label themselves as being "not enough" for a man are more likely to compromise their standards to avoid losing him.

2. Resist the urge to lose your cool and tell a man off. Immediately burning your bridges by acting out will only reaffirm what he already believes about you: That he can do better than you. Women who are prone to this sort of behavior are likely to lose out on *a lot* of great relationships

because they see male behavior as either being "good" or "bad." Human behavior isn't that simple, and in some cases, a gentle but firm reassertion of your boundaries (as opposed to a fierce outburst of your dissatisfaction) can quickly pull a man back to you.

Instead of succumbing to these powerless responses, become a master at reframing the negative into a positive when men do things you don't like. Try to see dating from his point of view and give him the guilt-free liberty to choose to be with you…or not. Assert your boundaries and stick to your standards, regardless of how desirable he is. And whenever a man seeks to lower your value by playing games or wasting your time, let him know that you appreciate who he is, that you're grateful for the time you shared together, and that even though he's incapable of making a woman like you happy, you want him to be happy anyway.

Responding like this illustrates the mark of a high-value woman, and it separates the girls from the women and the women from the irresistible sirens that make men desperate with devotion.

25

Even if you are plagued by much insecurity, you must still enforce upon yourself the dating habits of the kind of woman you wish to become. Habitually

acting as if you are a high-value woman will eventually make it so, even if you do not presently *feel* as if you are. Your true attractive power over men lies just beyond the intermittent discomforts that arise from refining your dating habits.

When a woman begins implementing the high value dating habits mentioned in this book, the biggest hindrance to her success will come from her own lack of self-confidence. If you have been single far longer than you care to remember, establishing clear boundaries with a highly desirable male specimen might make you feel terrified of losing out on a potential love interest. This is understandable. For most women, if they don't *feel* as if they possess the looks, personality, status, or regular male attention of a high-value woman, they feel especially challenged when an opportunity arises for them to act the part.

So, what is the solution to this confidence-deficit dilemma? Simple. Consistently act the part of the woman you wish to become, even if it feels "fake" and uncomfortable while doing it.

Interestingly, the adage to "fake it until you make it" actually has some truth to it. In modern psychology, there is a concept called **cognitive dissonance**. In the simplest terms, cognitive dissonance is the uncomfortable feelings we experience whenever we hold two or more contradictory beliefs about ourselves, or when we act in ways that are incongruent with our inner beliefs and values. When we have contradictory beliefs and behaviors, it creates an uncomfortable stress that forces us to seek internal consistency, either by changing the incongruous behavior or abandoning the inconsistent belief.

Knowing this, if you wish to adopt a new identity as a high-value woman, you must be willing to work through the cognitive dissonance you might experience as you strive for your new identity. You must be willing to consistently play the part of the woman you wish to become until your brain is forced to abandon those self-sabotaging beliefs that no longer serve you.

What I love about the human brain is that it will do everything in its power to close the gap between what you think about yourself and what your actions say about you. This is why your new identity as a high-value woman will not be a product of contemplation, meditation, or even just from reading a book. It will be a product of the quality of your habits. And your habits, as you probably already know, are simply the actions you take on a consistent basis. Change comes through action. Act. Become. Be willing to rinse and repeat this process until your brain is <u>forced</u> to give you the positive emotions you need to make your high-value behavior even more irresistible to men.

If you wish to generate the powerful self-belief that you are a high-value woman who is worthy of a man's unconditional love, you will need to accept the fact that the development of this belief will, at first, be an uncomfortable process. Whenever you establish a boundary or express your standards to a man, you must get over those misleading emotions that make you feel like you are lying to yourself or acting "fake." The more you act confidently with men, in spite of your inner uneasiness, the more confidence you will gain over time. Eventually, your brain will start providing you with the emotions that your actions have been <u>demanding</u> over the course of your behavior.

Give yourself the time to change into the woman you wish to become. Push through the fear, the insecurity, and ignore the mean girl inside your head who's always telling you that you're not pretty enough, tall enough, good enough, smart enough, young enough, feminine enough, outgoing enough, etc. Whenever the mean girl starts mouthing off all the ways in which you "suck", try to keep in mind that different men are attracted to very different things when it comes to a woman's looks, personality, and interests. This means that the same collection of qualities you think aren't "enough" might be the very collection of qualities your Mr. Right has been desperately trying to find in a single woman.

Don't worry about feeling as if you're "not enough" for a guy. You are enough. The more important thing is to ensure that you maintain your standards, confidently express your needs, and communicate your boundaries as you flirt, tease, and charm your way into a man's heart.

Remember, all men possess short-term and long-term mating strategies that run parallel to each other whenever they begin pursuing a woman. This means that the only way a guy can tell if you're a short-term pursuit or long-term relationship material is through experiencing your behavior. This is excellent news for a woman, as it means that once a guy is sincerely interested in her, he already thinks she's "enough." Her only job therefore, is to ensure that she embraces the dating behaviors of the high-value woman, as these are the behaviors that cultivate long-term attraction in men rather than short-term.

<u>Chapter Four:</u>

How to Capture His Heart and Bring Out His Best

26

Above all else, remember: It is the man's job to win you over, not the other way around. This is the cornerstone belief that separates women who are highly sought-after for love and commitment from those who are not.

Listen, I get it. To get ahead on your job, in college, or even in your business you've had to take the initiative in everything in order to get your needs met and achieve your goals. Adopting this particular approach to getting your needs met in these arenas has brought you a healthy amount of success, and thus, it's easy to assume that "taking the initiative" and being highly assertive in your love life should surely yield the same results. Unfortunately, this assumption couldn't be further from the truth when it comes to cultivating long-term attraction with men, especially highly masculine, relationship-minded men.

If you take the initiative in the beginning dating stages, you run the risk of turning men off. Men want to be the pursuers and are romantically wired to do so. Any initiatives you take to "spark things up" or move the relationship forward is a lost opportunity for the man you're dating. Yes, a high-quality man will consider himself a "prize-catch" to a phenomenal woman, but he doesn't want to be treated as such until he's done the initial legwork to assess your value and secure your affection. Only after some sort of consistent relationship has been established will a man truly appreciate your efforts to "win" his heart. Read that paragraph again.

Even if you think he's not moving "fast enough", do not take the initiative to move things forward or to see what his intentions are concerning you. As I mentioned before, although this sort of behavior will get you ahead in your career and business, it will hinder your success with men. If a man wants to be with you he will make his presence in your life both consistent and dominant. You won't have to chase him, check up on him, or call him to get closure. You will know based on his enthusiasm, attentiveness, and the amount of effort he takes to wedge himself into your life.

A man will always value that which he has worked to attain, especially when it comes to the woman he's dating. If he has to "win" her over, he will have satisfied his masculine need for a great romantic conquest. By feeling as if he's "won" her over he will also have greater confidence in the relationship, due to him knowing that the relationship itself was HIS idea.

When you make the man a "prize" that needs to be pursued, you run the risk of making him feel like *less* of a man. To him at least, it will feel as if you're trying to coerce him into a relationship. And when he feels as if he's being "sweetly" pressured into a commitment, your value as a long-term partner immediately drops in his eyes. This is one of the most common reasons why men pull away and suddenly disappear in the beginning stages of a blossoming romance.

No matter how far women have come in terms of socioeconomic equality with men, long-term attraction between the sexes will always be based on our most primal mating drives. Sure, over time culture can influence our courtship rituals and lead us into more "progressive" dating practices, but when it's all said and done, the things that make a man burn with white-hot desire for a woman cannot (and perhaps will not) be so easily changed by something as transitional as culture.

Remember, although men and women are considered equal, it does not mean that we are the same. To cultivate long-term attraction with a man, a woman must ensure that her dating habits are unlike his own and are more akin to the things men most treasure about her gender. In the beginning stages, men are more likely to respond to you on deep, primal level if you are warm, friendly, easy-to-please, kind, deferential to his leadership, and even **hesitant to commit**.

Remember, before a man can commit to you he needs to feel a strong emotional attraction to you. You can only cultivate this attraction by granting *him* the gift of chasing *you*. Keeping this firmly in mind will prevent you from taking on the dominant role (which is *his* role) in the beginning of a love affair, as only the woman who *knows* that she IS the "prize" can maintain this frame of attitude when interacting with a man.

27

Manners. Courtesy. Etiquette. Know what gentleman civility towards a woman looks like and how to incite it. The key to

arousing a man's more genteel demeanor is to give him the gift of proving to you that he is, in fact, better than any other man you could possibly have.

One of the most powerful things a woman can do to increase her mate value in the eyes of a man is to use her feminine wiles to graciously encourage him to treat her like a lady. Naturally, while a man's gentlemanly treatment will have more to do with his own level of refinement as well as his level of attraction to you, it's still *very* easy to lower your value in the eyes of such men if you neglect to reinforce the good behavior while rebuffing the negative ones. High-quality men want to know that you are familiar with gentlemanly refinement, that you appreciate it, and most importantly, that you *expect* it.

Some women are extremely hesitant towards encouraging men to treat them like ladies. This is mostly due to their fear of scaring away a potential boyfriend and/or husband. This fear of driving away a seemingly good man causes them to settle for subpar treatment, especially while out on dates or when communicating with men through text messaging. If you have a deep-rooted fear of driving men away that causes you to endure discourteous treatment...stop it.

Just...stop it.

You are more likely to gain a man's respect and adoration than his disapproval or disinterest whenever you're able to recognize and rebuff discourteous or inconsiderate behavior. Yes, this may sound counter-intuitive, but acting counter-intuitive (setting firm boundaries) to what we *think* will make people like us is what usually makes people like (respect) us. This is the very nature of attraction. Politely rebuffing discourteous and inconsiderate behavior tells a man that you respect yourself, that you're committed to protecting your dignity, and most importantly, it subconsciously tells him that you have become accustomed to being treated well by *other* men, perhaps men better than himself. Read that last sentence again.

Also, keep in mind that it is better for a woman to address unrefined male behavior early on than to endure it and try to correct it later. Don't get me wrong, I'm not saying you should nit-pick everything a guy does. For heaven's sake, do not nit-pick everything a guy does and do not try to chisel him into your Prince Charming. This is the other end of the spectrum, and it is these kinds of behaviors that WILL make a man run in the opposite direction. But with that said, I still encourage you to both recognize gentlemanly behavior towards a woman and develop the feminine communication skills needed to incite it.

The thing is, if you desire to be seen as a high value woman worthy of a man's unconditional love, then you need to convey to men that you are a lady and that you expect to be treated like one. For example, let's say you're going out on your fourth date with a guy and he has taken it upon himself to pick you up for the date. If he jumped out of his car but neglected to open your door for you, you would be in your perfect right if you simply sat there and waited for him to figure out why you're still in the car. Now, as you're sitting prettily in the passenger side, usually only one of three things are going to happen:

1. He will ask you what's the matter, apologize when you tell him, share a laugh about his

embarrassment, and then open your door with a heighten sense of adoration for you.

2. He will ask you what's the matter, maybe apologize (while rolling his eyes), and then open your door with at least a heightened sense of respect for you.

3. He will stubbornly walk into the restaurant...alone, at which point you will call a friend or taxi to take you home. And once you're on your way home, ensure that you promptly delete his contact from your phone.

Using these outcomes as general examples, I'm sure we can agree that being expectant and even insistent of being treated like a lady will help you weed out the good guys from the losers. It will make it easier for you to separate the often flawed but good-intentioned men from the immature narcissists who would rather walk away from a good thing than correct their own behavior.

Now, you may be wondering what some of the other gentlemanly behaviors look like. You may even be wondering when is it a good idea to address a behavior and when should a woman just let it go for the sake of making a connection. Well, because I'm a helpful gentleman myself, I've provided a short list of situations to look out for:

- If you are walking with your Prince Charming, ensure that you do not enter a door, car, or otherwise that he has not opened for you. You are a high-value woman and deserve to be ushered into places by a man who is willing to protect you and give the impression that are you cared for.

- If he's picking you up in his car and honks his

horn or calls your phone to get you to come to him...do not come to him. Politely inform him that it is customary for a gentleman to knock on a lady's door (or at least buzz her apartment) when picking her up for a date. If he reacts negatively, be done with him. If he apologizes and acquiesces, reward him with your amnesty and gratitude.

- If you're walking on a sidewalk together, pay attention to the side he walks on. One of the three pillars of manhood is *to protect*. Hence, if he is a man of refined masculinity, he will either quietly take the side closest to traffic or he will speak up and politely insist that he does. If he does nothing, don't immediately count it against him. Politely tell him that you "feel safer" walking on the other side of him and then take note of how he responds. Informing him that you "feel safer" at one side or another will subconsciously make him aware that *you* are aware of your preciousness and value as a woman. Your insistence in simple moments like this one can leave lasting impressions that will positively affect the way he treats you as the relationship progresses.

- If you're on a date and he consistently answers his phone or replies to texts, the next time he does so, say something flirty like this: *"Wow, that MUST be important if you'd rather talk to them than me!"* If this flirtatious exchange doesn't make a dent in his armor and change his behavior you might have to get a bit firmer.

The next time he disrupts the date with a phone interruption of any kind, politely excuse yourself.

If he does so again, excuse yourself a second time. Ensure that you make him wait a few minutes before returning, and keep your distance if he hasn't ended the interruption. After excusing yourself the second time, he should hopefully get the picture and from thereon forward resist answering his phone.

If he doesn't immediately get it and thus, asks why you keep excusing yourself, graciously let him know that you assume he's answering his phone for work or something else important and that you don't want to impose upon his privacy or divide his attention. If you're prone to being particularly sassy, you might even want to tell him something like this: *"I'm having a really great time with you, but I'm really not fond of sharing that time with your phone. I would much rather have you all to myself. That is, assuming of course, that you want me all to yourself as well."* (Make sure you're smiling and giving him the sassy, flirty eyes as you say this).

Now, if he's a red-blooded man with even an ounce of common sense, he'll understand the subtext of what you're saying and will then apologize about his offence and insist that it won't happen again. Remember, in most cases it's not what you say to a man, but *how* you say it that matters most. Assuming you choose your words graciously, men are more likely to respond positively when you set boundaries that let them know that their actions are out of line with what you are used to. Read that last sentence again.

Again, these are just a few situations to get your brain thinking in the right direction. Get together with your friends and try to come up with some examples of your own and how you should best respond to them, as I'm sure you and your girl friends have been on enough dates to experience the many unsavory flavors of male incivility.

Now, some modern-day women might think that expecting men to do things like open doors for them is nothing but silly "old-fashioned" patriarchal nonsense. If you so happen to fall into this group, let me gently attempt to shift your paradigm. You see, these seemingly "old-fashioned" gentlemanly gestures are based on the things that cultivate and sustain love and respect between men and women within romantic relationships. As I mentioned before, one of the three pillars of manhood is *to protect*, and a man is more likely to *feel* a strong emotional connection to a woman when she allows him to thrive in this masculine role.

Gentlemanly gestures like opening doors for a woman gives *us* a feeling of chivalry and power and makes us *feel* like protectors. It also gives us a feeling of importance because it burdens us with the responsibility of enhancing your dignity. This feeling of importance comes from us knowing that the better we treat you in public, the more your perceived value increases in the eyes of others. Knowing this makes us feel good in your presence, and thus, keeps us addicted to giving you first class treatment. Let that sink in.

Think about it. How many times have you sighed quietly and smiled to yourself when an elderly gentleman holds a door open for his wife and escorts her into a building? There is something deep within us all that makes us happy inside whenever a man and woman interact with one another in a way that makes a man appear chivalrous and a woman appear cherished.

So, if you want to quickly establish that you are something to be "cherished" by a man, you need to be both expectant and graciously insistent that you be treated like a lady. And so long as you're not nit-picking your Prince Charming at every turn, don't worry about scaring him away. Believe me, if a man has a sincere romantic interest in you, deep down inside he desperately wants to prove to you that he's the best thing to enter your life since you started wearing Spanx.

28

Let him lead, but follow at your own pace.

If you've read any of my other books you'll know that I'm a big proponent of letting a man lead when it comes to moving things forward in a relationship. Before an exclusive relationship has formed, he should be the one who initiates contact with you the most, not the other way around. He should be the one making concrete plans to spend time with you now and in the future. And he should be the one doing the chasing, as he makes the necessary sacrifices to ensure that his presence in your life is both consistent and dominant. However, even though it's his job to convince you of his commitment, it's your job to follow at a pace you find most comfortable.

As a man leads the progression of the relationship, you keep a comfortable pace with him by mainly doing two things:

1. Respecting your boundaries and your inhibitions. For example: If YOU don't feel comfortable committing to him just yet, even if he *seems* ready, willing, and able...don't.

2. Not acting overzealous to take yourself "off the market" for him.

One of the main benefits of following at your own pace is that it will keep you from coming on strong and thus, scaring guys away. By being reluctant, relaxed, and unhurried to get into a commitment, it makes you even more attractive to men; as such restrained behavior will speak volumes about your self-confidence and self-respect.

Men are fully aware that some women can become pretty excessive and even obsessive in their efforts to attain an exclusive relationship. Thus, being cautious and guarded, at least regarding a man's *initial* displays of passion towards you, is one of the keys to quickly connecting with him. Being slow to give-in to him keeps you off his "She's Commitment Crazy!" radar, which then makes it easier for him to open up and connect with you on a more emotional level.

Another key benefit of following at your own pace is that it keeps you from making mistakes of passion, as you can better judge a man's character and relationship goals when you give yourself time for him to reveal himself. The benefit here is that you will only "give in" to a man's advances when you've been thoroughly convinced that his actions concerning you are both sincere and reliable. A man might be sincere about his feelings concerning you, but that doesn't mean he's able to commit to you wholeheartedly, thus making him unreliable. And a man might be reliable in how he pursues you, but he may only be doing so to get something from you, thus he lacks sincerity.

Following at your own pace thus gives you the space and time necessary to properly evaluate both a man's character and his true intentions. If you allow yourself to get too easily swept up in the heat of a blossoming romance, you might wake up to realize that the man who so passionately pursued you in the beginning seems to no longer exist and wants nothing to do with you.

Contrary to popular belief, men get swept up by their passionate feelings and "fall in love" very quickly, but not necessarily permanently. Because of this, a man's display of insistent passion might convince (or seduce) you into believing that his feelings for you are a genuine representation of both his capacity for commitment and his desire to do so. Unfortunately, as many disgruntled women can attest, once you prematurely "give in" to a man's passions he quickly loses interest and eventually disappears.

If you have ever experienced this for yourself, you were probably left feeling confused, irritated, insulted, and even dumbfounded. Especially if something (your female intuition) warned you not to fall for him so quickly and told you that you should have waited a little bit longer before giving him what he *seemed* to want so badly. The key to avoiding this sort of situation is to manage his passion by simply refusing to get swept up in it. In other words, your power over a man's romantic desire lies in the strength of your own restraint.

You see, when a woman reciprocates our romantic interest while maintaining an air of restraint, this communicates her high self-respect. It tells us that she either has or could have other options out there. It also tells us that she doesn't want to take herself off the market prematurely.

To the man who isn't that interested in you or who isn't totally sure about you, following him at your own pace will drive him away as he'll consider you to be "too much work." **This is a good thing, and you should consider yourself fortunate when romantically-lazy and opportunistic men consider you a waste of time.** However, to the man who REALLY wants you, following his lead at your own pace will make him even *more* determined to have you all to himself and deeply grateful when he finally does. Remember that.

29

Do not neglect the power of a woman's *preciousness*. Men are naturally driven to protect and possess that which emanates preciousness. The woman who makes herself *precious* to men will quickly find herself overwhelmed with attention from male suitors who are stubborn in their love and determined in their devotion.

In the most primal sense, a woman risks her health, safety, and the future well-being of herself and her offspring when choosing a man to give her all to. For a man however, when deciding on a woman to give his all to, he risks his resources, his social status, and the future likelihood that the offspring he raises will be his. Those risks are very REAL and terrifying, and it's something women will never truly understand. And it's these risks that make a lot of men extremely skittish about long-term commitment.

Fortunately, one of the best ways to help a man overcome this skittishness regarding commitment is to communicate "preciousness." If you were really paying attention you might have realized that every one of the guidelines mentioned within this book will help you to communicate your preciousness to the men you date.

When interacting with a man, a woman will always get the best results when she maintains a feminine frame of mind. When a woman possesses a feminine frame of mind, she is less likely to falter or lose her comportment when a man does things that either threaten her dignity or make her seem unimportant. Maintaining a feminine frame of mind allows her to communicate "preciousness" to a man, and thus, if he is a high-quality man, it *forces* him to treat her with respect and adoration. On the other hand, if the man in question has malicious intent or just isn't right for her, the "preciousness" she communicates to him will *chase* him away.

This is why you must internalize this belief: *"I am precious to men."*

Write this phrase out somewhere and place it where you can view it daily. Repeat it to yourself during those moments of self-doubt and self-loathing. Even amid subpar male treatment, let this phrase dominate your thoughts so that your response to such treatment will be that of a high-value, dignified woman. Don't allow your own insecurities or your past relationship failures to define your present interactions with men. Internalize the belief that as a woman, by birthright, *you are precious to men*. Successfully internalizing this belief has the potential to transform your love life for the better.

For a man interacting with a woman, the masculine frame of mind must communicate his <u>necessity</u> to her well-being and his <u>indomitability</u> in the face of her rebuffs. Thus, for a man to succeed in the game of dating and mating, his essence, his very aura must convey the belief that: *"I am essential to women."* When a man's speech, body language, and personality become infused by this belief, it makes him way more attractive to the opposite sex and thus, increases his success at finding a high-value mate of his own.

When a man knows his worth and shows his indomitableness in the midst a woman's tests, rebuffs, and negative emotions, it does something to her on a primal level. She cannot help but feel a deep respect for him, and in most cases, her attraction to him skyrockets. This is exactly what happens to a man when a woman successfully communicates her *preciousness* to him. He cannot help but feel a deep respect and adoration for her, which then makes her even more attractive and worth whatever sacrifices he must make to have her and keep her in his life.

I mention all this to show you that men also have insecurities to overcome, and how a simple shift in a man's thinking can transform his love life. As a man, the more I like myself, regardless of what a woman thinks of me, the better chance I have at attracting phenomenal women to date.

But in practical terms, what does *preciousness* look like exactly? Well, listed below are a few examples of women who have internalized this empowering belief:

- Preciousness is the woman who confidently and tactfully declines a man's invitation to spend the night at his place, knowing full well that he may never call her again.

- Preciousness is the woman who ends an almost-relationship with a handsome doctor after realizing that she's the only one interested in progressing the relationship.

- Preciousness is the young woman who has already decided that she doesn't French kiss guys who aren't her boyfriend, and follows through on that personal decision, regardless of the men or situation.

- Preciousness is the woman who forces herself not to call a guy after he begins showing clear signs of a loss of interest.

- Preciousness is the woman who uses her silent behavior to incite a man to treat her with kindness, compassion, and gentleman civility.

- Preciousness is the woman who ignores a man's on-again off-again flirtatious texting after going on two dates with him three months ago and never being asked out again.

- Preciousness is the woman who is immediately turned off when a man wants her to come over for Netflix and "chill" as a first, second, or third date.

- Preciousness is the woman who refuses to use sex as a means to keep men interested in her.

- Preciousness is the young woman who gives men

the freedom to *choose* her…or not; meaning that if faced with a withdrawing man she will not attempt to change his mind, chase him, or guilt-trip him using passive aggression.

- Preciousness is the woman who is vulnerable and sincere, even in the face of rejection; meaning that if faced with a withdrawing man she will admit to her deep feelings for him but still let him choose to *not* be with her if that is what he so desires.

- Preciousness is the woman who prioritizes her dignity and communicates her boundaries by making it very clear that she will not "wait around" for a man to return to her if he wishes to date other women. **And she will follow up on this promise by making herself available to date other men.** She also makes it clear that she will not engage in a "casual", uncommitted romantic relationship with him if he desires to "go on a break" or end their current relationship.

- Preciousness is the woman who appreciates a man's honesty regarding his interest in her and makes it clear that she'd rather they be happy apart than to be stuck together and unable to meet each other's needs.

- Preciousness is the woman who perceives a man's rejection as his inability to meet *her* needs, NOT the other way around.

- Preciousness is the woman who does nice things for her new guy not because she wants him to like her, but simply because that is who she is.

Each of these examples are preciousness in action, and as you can see, they have nothing to do with a woman being "nice" or sweet. Don't confuse being precious with being sweet or nice to a man. Chances are, you're reading this book because you realize that being the "nice girl" hasn't been working for you to get the relationship you want.

The thing is, the problem with being "too nice" is that it's a *seemingly* attractive but ultimately poor strategy for communicating preciousness. You might think that by being overly nice and accommodating you're more likely to gain the good graces of the men you date. Unfortunately, as you've probably realized by now, the "super-nice-super-sweet" dating strategy will make you an attractive target for players, a fun plaything for time wasters, and mere collateral damage for men who meant well at first, but who ultimately lost their attraction to you.

Having well-established personal boundaries, reasonable dating standards, and a determination to be treated with unconditional love is the only way to communicate preciousness to a man. By internalizing the belief that men want to claim you as their own because you are essential to their happiness, you will breathe new life into your interactions with men and make yourself more attractive to the right man. Remember, a man will embrace the beliefs you hold about yourself. If you *believe* and thus, act as if you are exquisite and valuable to men, you will soon find yourself being treated as such. Guaranteed.

Final Thoughts

One of the most crucial things to remember when it comes to attracting the relationship you want is to adopt the mindset that while you might *want* a particular guy to be your boyfriend you don't *need* him to be your boyfriend. If you can understand and internalize this single very important concept it will make assimilating the knowledge in this book exceptionally easy for you. (Seriously, let this belief *sink* into your subconscious and you'll be surprised at how easy it is to uphold your standards with the men you date.)

When it comes to your personal beliefs, meeting a particular guy should not be a precursor to "the life you've always wanted." Seeing some guy you've been out with a handful of times as "the man of your dreams" will tempt you to lower your standards when he starts to act in ways that don't make you happy. Harboring these internal beliefs will be destructive to your efforts to attract the relationship you want. Why? Well, mainly because attracting the kind of man you really want requires womanly poise and power, two things that can only exist when a woman doesn't feel as if having a particular guy in her life will answer all of her problems.

Also, if you're especially prone to having Nice Girl tendencies, you must learn to let go and let men lead in

111

order to really succeed with men and dating. Instead of caving in and compromising your standards to make a guy like you, focus on strengthening his emotional attraction to you by maintaining your standards, connecting with his heart, and most importantly, giving up your need to control the trajectory of the relationship. The need for control is a self-sabotaging habit for the Nice Girl, as she often tries to regulate the trajectory of a relationship by making things easy for a guy, chasing him when he loses interest, doing girlfriend-like favors for him, or even using sex as a way to keep him interested.

Instead of letting your niceness dictate your behavior, focus on being "the heart" of the relationship and allow your new potential beau the opportunity to prove that he can be "the head" of the relationship. I know, I know. If you haven't been raised in an environment where your father or some other male authority figure made you feel loved and secure through his brand of leadership, accepting this concept will be difficult. However, I implore you to give it a try.

You can only be sure of a man's love if he is making a concerted effort to "lead" the relationship. I repeat: you can only be sure of a man's love if he is making a concerted effort to "lead" the relationship. This is why you *must* focus on being "the heart" and allow him to prove himself to you. If you insist on taking control of things as you attempt to win his heart, over time, chances are you will only end up winning his contempt. It is impossible for a woman to force a man's interest and commit to her by trying to negotiate his desire.

As I've mentioned in the introduction, desire cannot be negotiated. A man cannot negotiate your desire to get you to go out with him, have sex with him, to spend more time with him, or to fall in love with him, and the same applies for women. A man will not respond to your tears, tantrums, begging, or nagging, at least, not in the way you want him to. And he most certainly will not respond favorably to you if you willingly become his doormat.

What he *will* respond to however, are your reasonable, personal standards, your tenderness with his ego, the fearlessness of your love, and your womanly poise. As you can see, these are all things that you have FULL control over, as they are the qualities of the self-possessed, high-value woman who deserves the unconditional love of a good man.

Doormats don't arouse a man's devotion, and thus, they end up in dead-end relationships more often than they'd like. But the woman with class and character, one who expects to be treated like a priceless and *precious* treasure, is the one who will easily capture a man's desire and make him crave her closeness, her companionship, and her ultimate commitment. Remember that.

By the way...

As a way of saying "thanks" for your purchase, I'm offering a free 10-lesson email course (and other assorted goodies) that are exclusive to my book readers. Each lesson reveals some of my best-kept dating secrets for cultivating long-term attraction with high-quality men.

You can access it at:

http://www.brucebryans.com/ecourse/

In this free course you will learn the most attractive dating habits of high-value women; the kind of women that make men burn with desire and desperate to commit to them. You will also discover the secrets to having more confidence and power with men and dating so that you can get the guy you want, keep him interested, and quickly weed out the time-wasters, the players, and the men who'll never commit.

In this knowledge-packed course, you'll discover:

- How to stand your ground and confidently communicate your boundaries in a way that INCREASES a man's attraction to you instead of turning him off.

- The one thing you absolutely MUST do when the man you love and want begins to pull away from you in a relationship.

- How to quickly hook Mr. Right from the first few dates by doing something MOST women are terrified of doing after meeting a great guy.

- What to do when a man says he "loves you" but he doesn't call you enough (or perhaps even at all).

- The #1 key to conquering the masculine heart and how to use this knowledge to cultivate DEEP feelings of love in a man. (Hint: This is the fastest way to tap into a man's emotional needs and make him see you as "Girlfriend Material.")

- A simple way to SKYROCKET your chances of meeting Mr. Right instead of desperately waiting for a "stroke of luck" to change your love life.

- And much, much more…

Enter the web address below into your Internet browser and join the thousands of other women who have used these attraction secrets to get more confidence, power, and results with men and dating.

Again, you can access it at:

http://www.brucebryans.com/ecourse/

See you on the inside,

Bruce

Before you go...

I just wanted to say "thank you" for purchasing my book.

I know you could have picked from dozens of books on understanding men, but you took a chance on my guide and for that I'm extremely grateful. So, thanks again for purchasing this book and reading all the way to the end.

Now, if you liked this book, **please take a minute or two to leave a review for it on Amazon so that other women just like you can find out more about it**. Your feedback is most appreciated as it helps me to continue writing books that get you results.

And "thank you" in advance for your review. I am eternally grateful.

Dating & Attraction Books by Bruce Bryans:

Below is a list of my books for women that you can find on Amazon.com. You can easily find them all here at: http://www.amazon.com/author/brucebryans

***

Texts So Good He Can't Ignore: Sassy Texting Secrets for Attracting High-Quality Men (and Keeping the One You Want)

In *Texts So Good He Can't Ignore*, you'll discover how to use texting to easily create attraction with your guy and finally get him OFF of his smartphone and ON more dates with you.

Never Chase Men Again: 38 Dating Secrets to Get the Guy, Keep Him Interested, and Avoid Dead-End Relationships

In *Never Chase Men Again*, you'll learn how to get the guy you want, train him to pursue you, and avoid dead-end or even "dead-on-arrival" relationships by being more assertive and communicating high-value to the men you date.

How To Get A Man Without Getting Played: 29 Dating Secrets to Catch Mr. Right, Set Your Standards, and Eliminate Time Wasters

In *How To Get A Man Without Getting Played*, you'll discover the beliefs, attitudes, dating rules, "love habits", and seduction secrets high-value women use to eliminate time wasters and find Mr. Right.

He's Not That Interested, He's Just Passing Time: 40 Unmistakable Behaviors of Men Who Avoid Commitment and Play Games with Women

In *He's Not That Interested, He's Just Passing Time*, you'll learn how to read a man's behavior to find out if he wants a relationship with you or if he's just leading you on and completely wasting your time.

Never Get Ghosted Again: 15 Reasons Why Men Lose Interest and How to Avoid Guys Who Can't Commit

In *Never Get Ghosted Again*, you'll discover the secret reasons why men lose interest, what causes men to fall in and out of love, and how to prevent great guys from disappearing on you.

The 7 Irresistible Qualities Men Want In A Woman: What High-Quality Men Secretly Look for When Choosing "The One"

In *The 7 Irresistible Qualities Men Want In A Woman*, you'll discover the feminine qualities that commitment ready, high-quality men look for when choosing a long-term mate.

Make Him BEG For Your Attention: 75 Communication Secrets for Captivating Men and Getting the Love and Commitment You Deserve

In *Make Him BEG For Your Attention*, you'll discover how to talk to a man so that he listens to you, opens up to you, and gives you what you want without a fuss.

Dating Deal Breakers That Drive Men Away: 12 Relationship Killers That Ruin Your Long-term Potential with High-Quality Men

In *Dating Deal Breakers That Drive Men Away*, you'll learn the most common dating red flags that high-quality men consider "deal-breakers", the kind of deal-breakers that compel them to stop pursuing a woman, ignore her texts (and phone calls), and eventually blow up a budding relationship.

Send Him A Signal: 61 Secrets for Indicating Interest and Attracting the Attention of Higher Quality Men

In *Send Him A Signal*, you'll learn the subtle signs of female interest that entices men to pursue a woman and also how to become more approachable to high-quality guys.

101 Things Your Dad Never Told You About Men: The Good, Bad, and Ugly Things Men Want and Think About Women and Relationships

In *101 Things Your Dad Never Told You About Men*, you'll learn what high-quality men want from women and what they think about love, sex, and romance. You'll learn how to seduce the man you want or captivate the man you love because you'll know exactly what makes him tick.

101 Reasons Why He Won't Commit To You: The Secret Fears, Doubts, and Insecurities That Prevent Most Men from Getting Married

In *101 Reasons Why He Won't Commit To You*, you'll learn the most common fears, doubts, and insecurities that paralyze men and prevent them from making the leap from boyfriend to husband.

About Bruce Bryans

Bruce Bryans is a successful author with a passion for research into the dating and mating rituals of men and women. He doesn't fashion himself as some all-knowing "relationship guru", but instead prefers to provide insightful information based on the social and biological factors that bring men and women together for love and romance. Bruce has written numerous books on topics including: masculinity, attraction, dating strategy, and gender dynamics within romantic relationships. Bruce's main aim is to provide easy-to-implement, practical information that helps men and women improve their dating market value and mating desirability to the opposite sex.

When he isn't tucked away in some corner writing a literary masterpiece (or so he thinks), Bruce spends most of his time engaged in manly hobbies, spending time with friends, or being a lovable nuisance to his wife and children.

You can learn more about his writings and receive updates (and future discounts) on his books by visiting his website at: www.BruceBryans.com

Share the Secrets

If you've been empowered, enlightened, or helped in any way by this book, please recommend it to your sisters, daughters, co-workers, and friends. If you're a blogger or fellow author, consider recommending it to your readers. And if you're a dating coach, therapist, counselor, etc., and you strongly believe that this book can help your clients, please consider recommending it to them or purchasing copies to give away as gifts.

I sincerely hope this book does wonders not only for your love life, but for the lives of the women you care about as well.

Here's to your success!

Bruce Bryans

Made in the USA
Coppell, TX
20 June 2020